AF662789

A WALK

Tread on Champ

notionpress.com

A WALK

Tread on Champ

YUVRAJ HUMAN

notionpress.com

Notion Press

Old No. 38, New No. 6

McNichols Road, Chetpet

Chennai - 600 031

First Published by Notion Press 2015

ISBN 978-93-5206-527-1

DEDICATION

I wish to dedicate this book to my mentor, the third President of Soka Gakkai, Dr. Daisaku Ikeda and every single member of Bharat Soka Gakkai. Sensei, keeping you in my heart I have improved and will constantly improve and become more a compassionate and courageous person. I vow to do my best as your disciple, come what may.

FOREWORD

It was about 8 AM on a hot summer's day, the bell signalling the end of classes had just been rung. As scheduled, a friend and I were preparing to conduct interviews for recruiting freshers into the Leadership Training Service, a movement based on mentorship. Little did we know what was going to hit us. This rugged looking man walked up and took the chair. After a few preliminary questions and answers, he opened up to tell the story of his life thus far. Both of us, interviewing him, were left spellbound and speechless. We felt like raising our hands in a salute. We ended up hugging him instead. This man was Yuvraj, and I am elated that, in the following pages, he will reveal his story to you like he did to us that morning.

It is the story of a 15 year old boy standing by the railway tracks who, while contemplating suicide, decides to turn his life around and take on the battle against poverty, pain, and his initial desire to quit. This is not a figment of someone's imagination. It is the true story of a man who changed his destiny, what we call the 'ultimate writing on the wall', through his continued perseverance despite all odds. It is also the story of aspirational India, of unprecedented times in the country when the willingness to achieve dreams is slowly, but surely, meeting its apt fulfillment, of the rising dawn where the journey, the Walk matters more than the destination itself.

At the end of the story, you will take back inspiration to last a lifetime and say to yourself, 'Yes, I can do it!'. Even you can walk the Walk, even you can live your dream. You will experience a roller coaster of emotions as you read along, but rest assured, this man will turn it around to make you believe in yourself. Remember, what you read here is not just words: it is a documentation of a person, just like you and I, yet so different from everyone around him, who said "No" to his discouraging circumstances and went on to live his dream.

Sumesh Dugar is founder and CEO at Webbies, a company that is hard at work to bring emotional intelligence to modern computing.

Acknowledgements

I express my sincere gratitude to my indomitable mother and my diligent father. Without your love and care this book would not have become a reality. To my dearest brother, Jitendra, for your unconditional love and support. My dearest and closest friend, Pranam – thank you for standing by me. I also want to thank my dearest friends since my school days namely, Pankaj, Sidharth and Nitika.

I also want to express my utmost appreciation to Prayush for giving this book direction and helping me in making it a reality. I am also very thankful to Dr. Priya

Virmani for her enabling editing of this manuscript while ensuring my voice remained entirely intact.

Last but not the least, I am very much indebted to every member of Bharat Soka Gakkai who has selflessly helped me reflect on my shortcomings and work upon them. Through their support I constantly seek to better myself with each day.

Jubilant thanks to Paint Our World (POW), the NGO that works in the form of a life affirming humanitarian project, providing healing to underprivileged children who have been through the trauma of becoming orphaned, rape and child sexual abuse. I feel empowered to be part of the POW family. The message of this book chimes with the underpinning of POW – to celebrate our resilience, our ability to heal, to laugh and to love, the ability to overcome the odds a better not bitter person. Thank you Priya for taking me to the children. Should you, the reader, wish to link arms with POW look them up on social media or email info@paintourworld.org.

Hey Champ! How's it going? Are you looking for a much needed break or is it that the girl or boy you are in love with has broken your heart? What's disturbing you?

I call you a champ not to overwhelm you. You indeed are one. However, our deluded minds don't allow us to believe so, thanks to the trivial matters that seem to invariably bring our spirits down. It is because of these reasons that we either try to escape such instances or look for somebody who will be sympathetic towards us or look for a punching bag – perhaps someone we can hurtle abuses towards and displace our aggression on. We do this to others for no fault of theirs. Rather we do this in the belief that doing so will make us feel better, will make our problems go away? But does that really help us?

With devices, they become obsolete and eventually their value depletes. It is not so with life. At times, we live because we have to and discovering the purpose of life all but takes a backseat. Discovering the purpose of life is only possible if we face reality and travel through the experience of life's vicissitudes. This travelling categorically means to walk the walk you started at some point in your life, believing that even if today was the worst possible, tomorrow could see a shift and can bring a series of opportunities.

I feel a debt of gratitude for the myriad experiences I encountered – I kept falling, kept making mistakes, felt depressed and at times asked myself if committing suicide was the best option. Whenever I felt so, I would go to a railway track to wait for the train to come but I couldn't muster up the will to end my life. The fear of getting knocked down by the train and being pulverized into pieces terrified me.

Many amongst you, during your worst times, may have experienced what I felt then. The reason why I feel moments like these are revelatory is because it was me who went through all this and, most importantly, it was me who dealt with it. At such times, life to me appeared to be uncompromisingly brutal. Anxious moments were there in plenty. People around me seemed much happier and I felt jealous of their happiness. I yelled at myself in frustration. I could see myself getting crushed every single time I wanted to stand up. My childhood was over before it even began. The prime reason for all of this was the scarcity of money.

From the time I was 10, I saw my father going from one job to other. He was not very educated but despite this he was the most sought after salesman by good companies in Nepal. It was his ego that led him to quitting jobs and starting up his own business for a short span but all of that failed.

When my friends at school would plan an outing, I would become anxious because I knew that even though I wanted to go with them Papa would not have the cash to allow my participation. It was my adamant nature that would compel my father to give me money at any cost. Somehow, he would arrange for it and let me go.

I did not realize the extent of the financial pain my father was battling. If I talk of school fees, they were paid but not regularly. And it did not end there. People, to whom he owed a lot of money, kept knocking at our doors. He would often hide himself inside the kitchen or go outside for some time till the creditor would leave.

For my family and me, it felt like the stage was being set for troubles ahead. The turning point was when I was in class 10 preparing for my boards, that is, my school leaving exams. Years of financial trouble meant we were forced to flee Kathmandu. Even our landlord was not notified.

We sought refuge in our village where my brother and I started selling potatoes for a living. After sometime, we even sold fertilizers. All this selling was happening after my mother's ornaments were kept as collateral with a wealthy man in our village. Yet, things were looking bleak for us and we headed to Calcutta in the hope that our prospects there would be better. I worked as a laborer at a computer shop in Chandni Chowk and this continued for approximately a month before my mother sought financial assistance from the community people and got my younger brother and me admitted to a government school. I was now studying in class 9. Even my mother started working at a *saree* shop. There were times when our dinner comprised of *chapattis* and onions.

At 15, my circumstances were very different from that of a conventional 15 year old's life. But today, as I look back, it was those experiences of hardship that shaped me, that made me who I am today. The steel in me was forged during those arduous times. Even though we were being educated, there were things I could not ignore. Working part time at a friend's shop or looking for old books that I could use to study or shoes that I could borrow from someone else to be eligible to go to school, were harsh realities I endured. During my class 12 exams, I was fighting a battle to snatch something awesome, which a kid like me could never think of. Why? It was all because deep down I felt that now for me, there was nothing to lose and everything to gain. Day and night seemed to be the same. I did get into something amazing but it was tough to hold on to it.

My life at college was friend-less as I always found schisms between my batchmates and myself. To even think that I could match the other students or do as well as them was a farsighted dream for me.

Before getting into college, somewhere I had this thought at the back of my mind that if I do something splendid, then I would be able to see joy on my parents' faces and differences with my father would end but nothing happened as I had hoped. My father's behavior with me at home compelled me to take up a job at a call center. No one at home appreciated this move.

I would leave for college at 4 am and return home around 11:25 pm. My family members would be sleeping when I would leave home and when I would return. To be honest I didn't have time for anybody, not even for myself. In college, teachers would ask me to leave because I would sleep in class. No teacher likes such behaviour. I understood why the teachers would reproach me and hence without defending myself, I would quietly walk out of the class.

I always wanted to be with people with whom I could share my feelings. I resorted to counseling too. However, all of it was in vain. I got into a relationship presuming that a hand on a hand would make us strong enough to face the rest of the world. How foolish was I? The best thing in my life was my mother, who although occupied with her household and office work heard me time and again. When I began a relationship with a girl, in less than a month, she became my world. All of this had to end because she was really after casual fun and not any kind of serious commitment, which is what I was looking for.

Parents tell their children about recent happenings in the world, gift them new gadgets and games and take them on holidays. I knew nothing of this world. What I knew, was how to survive on Rs. 5 a day, how to fool the bus conductor and reach my destination without paying a single penny, how to sneak through the glasses of Café Coffee Day and get a glimpse of the match that was being shown on the LCD Screen and, most importantly, how to save money so that I could treat myself to a *samosa* or some *pani puri*. The worlds of my peer group and myself were different, as were our minds. So, when my peers spoke of gadgets, mobile phones, play stations or any English film, I would walk away from there with a dumb look on my face. If they spoke about going to a place or party somewhere, I would run away from there not because I did not want to join them but because I feared that they would find out about my financial state.

While all of this was going on, I formed a friendship with this man, whom I call by myriad names. It was not only one side advising the other but both of us contributed to the other's life in such a way that we cherished the times we met. Our families wondered if we were becoming a gay couple but we were more than that. We were buddies who would meet impromptu. We were friends who smoked in every corner of the city. We connected meaningfully.

Our friendship was not encouraged by our parents, yet we remained friends. Whenever I had no money to hang out with him, he would make sure that everything was being taken care of. I did feel bad when he did all this. There was a day when I told him to stop spending money on me like this because it reminds me of how poor I am. His reply won my heart forever. He said, "Don't worry, when you start earning I will take double the sum I am spending on you and you'll be the one treating me for lunch or anything else".

After graduation, it was time to prepare for competitive exams or to get a job. My friend and I, both chose the former. Our choice was not backed by any concrete action. We were not preparing like most people do. I was not that good at academics. With every mock test that I took, including the CAT, I scored poorly and this was also the case when I gave the CAT exam. My friend was more cerebral and that is why he scored well but the fact that I did not do well made him feel bad and that's when he suggested, that with the kind of scores we had, we take up admission in any decent college. I was ready but I had no backing from home. There were no arrangements for money at all and even thinking of an MBA seemed wasteful. Even at that point it was my father who tried out all options available and made sure my dream to pursue a MBA became a reality. Finally, I got through a MBA college in Gurgaon while my closest buddy got through an MBA college in Hyderabad.

We went and we vowed as friends that we shall do our best to stay connected. In a nutshell, I can sum up the MBA course that I pursued in Gurgaon as one which gave a new, invigorating direction to my life and made me become a man of conviction, a man of self belief.

All of this was only possible because of the relentless effort everyone at home was putting in to helping me in all ways.

So, now you would think that it was all so simple. However, for me it was not easy at all. Everything that came my way took many things away from me which, like would be the case with anyone made me feel horrible. However, that was all in the short run. In the long run all had to be well.

Why am I pausing now to write this book? Why do I want people to know about my life? There are so many questions that come to my mind and for them I don't have any spontaneous or easy answers. Yet, as I continue writing,

I am convinced that all the most important answers that I am looking for will be found.

Many of us love going through stories in a very organized way. Real life stories are not of that kind. My desire is to let this book be one of a kind. I don't want people to come up with generalized opinions about this book. Everyone must have something different to talk about after reading this book. Most importantly, I wish this book to touch the hearts of the people who read it.

I don't seek any publicity from this book. By journeying with this book if some of you start believing from your heart that even if today you lost, you have a new day awaiting you – life is full of surprises be they bad or good and that you won't yield, only then will my sole purpose of writing this book, be successful.

Actually, it is nothing but your inner choice to either say, I quit or get yourself moving and give it a fight, saying to yourself come on champ you are the one... Truly, you ARE the one.

Everyone travels on life's journey but how you travel is the important choice you make. Here it's crucial to make a decision to let our choice be governed by the spirit of a champ and not that of a coward. While I am being passionate about what I am saying, I also understand that it is easier said than done. For instance, you read something inspirational especially during a trying time in your life and decide to embark on fire fighting your travails with the spirit of a champ, then treading consistently on this path is paramount. It is commonplace that despite being resolute you dither when setbacks keep rearing their ugly heads.

I am an ordinary child of extraordinary parents. The reason why I say so is not because of what they were able to give me but for the kind of people they are. They are people who have constantly shown me, what an attitude of persevering with optimism can do. Perseverance nears you towards perfection and your goals. If I learnt this habit and I am continuing to learn, then the credit for this goes to them.

In 2003 when we decided to leave Kathmandu for India it was the time of the autumnal festival of Durga Puja. We were in a situation where we had everyone knocking on our doors, asking for money. Papa was under serious pressure. He went out every morning to find ways to repay the debts he owed.

At school I would hide myself from the eyes of the Principal because I knew that if he saw me, he would call me into his office and ask for the unpaid school fees. It was always out of fear that I would duck from the Principal as he hardly ever called me up for the unpaid fees. At that time I also started developing a habit of being scared when people knocked at our door to ask for any kind of payment.

I was 14 years old then. My mother was working hard to feed us. Papa was mired in such trouble that he could not handle it anymore. He was fed up of hiding inside the kitchen or balcony to keep away from creditors. Furthermore, his debtors never responded positively to him. Things were getting worse with each passing day. Then came a day when one of these creditors hit Papa hard on his face. My father had a sharp scissor behind him and was about to hit back at him but he dropped the idea in less than a second. After that man went away, Papa told us why he did not hit him back. He said if he would have hit him, the police would have taken him to jail after which his children would be deprived of a father.

This horrifying incident left us shocked and scared us as a family. Each one of us at home including my younger brother and my mother were of the opinion that we should leave this city and go to our village. In other words, our time in Kathmandu was soon to come to an end.

I have this habit of trying to analyse incidents in my life to extrapolate the lessons from it. Even at your worst you need to be aware of your responsibilities towards those closest to you such as your family and friends and to society at large. I presume all parents are of the same intent. When inspiration and motivation are needed, parents can be a guiding force. I realise the idea of fleeing was not empowering but it was the best in the given context.

We always have this habit of seeing the worst as something evil that's befallen us but when its gone we either forget about it or we say, "Somehow I managed to deal with it". When struck by such horrifying times even I did the same but today when I look back at myself, I realize that I have come a long way in life and now very rarely does anything perturb me. Deal with your woes not with a sad demeanor but that smiles through adversity. In case, you find yourself unable to do so then try this out. Go to a playground or a park and ask yourself, "How do I look when I smile?" Trust me, this strategy works. This does not mean that you are ignoring your problems. It actually means that you are ready to face and overcome your challenges.

It took us one week to pack our bags and leave Kathmandu. We left Kathmandu in a way that no one should ever have to leave a place. Landlord, neighbours, relatives and friends at school, none of them came to know of how and when we left the city, the city I was born and raised in.

We fled to our village in India where we had an ancestral home. Luckily, we had not sold it or we would have had no roof over our head anywhere. The initial days in the village were fairly pleasant. We have a big family who stay in nuclear units in the same village.

While all of them seemed happy about our settling in the village, my mother was not happy. She was desperate to help me give my board exams in Kathmandu. However, that was not to happen.

There is a season in which many shop owners in my village sell potatoes, basically to the farmers who use these potatoes as seeds – to grow more of them. I was very excited and eager to do the same. We did not have money to do so. My mother was never in support of this. Her entire effort was geared towards enabling me to give my board exams.

My father convinced my mother about our idea of getting into the business of selling potatoes. She reluctantly accepted the idea. My mother gave her ornaments to a moneylender as collateral in lieu of which we got money. This allowed us to use the area in front of our house as a hawker type shop where my younger brother and I would sit. We got potatoes from the wholesalers and started selling them on a daily basis.

My brother Jitu and I would wake up at 6 am, start cleaning the area, and get everything ready before the farmers started coming. Once the selling would start, it would not stop. My relatives were also into the same business. They feared our presence and wanted us to stop selling potatoes because we were giving them competition. They started taunting us, at times they would intentionally scream a lower price of potatoes and we would react to it by selling our potatoes at still lower prices. This was one way of trying to get us to leave the work we had just begun.

In the world of business where short term benefits are of prime importance, you end up using tactics which though not illegal, are unethical especially when meted out to you by your very own family members. Both, my brother and I, were clueless about how to succeed with this business. We saw nearby sellers starting to sell fertilizers. My brother and I thought of taking that up too. We both thought that if we start selling fertilizers then we would be able to attract more people to buy potatoes from us. What we were not aware of yet was the price.

The margins that these shopkeepers played on was more or less a percent of the cost incurred on a 50 kg pack of fertilizer. We were foolish to start selling fertilizers because the gap between the cost and the profit one made out of it was slim. My mother on the other hand began her tailoring work in the village. Even in her case, the money she made was very little as prices of stitched clothes were a lot cheaper in the village as compared to the city. So, to become competitive in the village she had to reduce her rates too.

My father was helping my mother in getting orders from various clothes shops. One would feel that things had started moving well. This was not happening so fast for us. After a couple of months, we found that our capital invested was getting exhausted. We now had no money to pay our creditors. We were always in search of money. We started eating food cooked in the old fashioned stoves in villages. It might seem like, with this part of my story in particular, fact might be coming across as stranger than fiction but I am merely narrating what actually happened.

Things in life happen when you least expect it or when you expect it the most. Anything can go wrong anytime. This is why we become so vulnerable. How uncertain our lives are? It was not long before when I was in Kathmandu and partying with friends and today I was in a village and wondering if I can even get a proper meal to eat.

I could see my own relatives backing out fearing that helping us would be of no benefit to them. I used to hear stories from my mother of how generously my father would give away money to relatives when they were in need. Why do people forget someone's good deeds towards them?

We were in the village for seven months when my mother took the bold step of calling up her elder brother in Calcutta expressing her concern about Jitu and my futures. I saw her weep while on the phone. Seeing my mother cry, I realized how hurt she was and decided I would do my best not to bring tears to her eyes.

She did not see any future for both her children in the village and it was because of her strong inner resolve to get my brother and me educated that today we both are well educated. Now that I am educated, I feel a profound sense of appreciation towards my mother who has been my greatest teacher. I learnt from my mother to strengthen my resolve to achieve my goals. Resolve, is key to realizing your dreams. I must admit that I wasn't often prudent and tended to worry a lot which wasn't always useful. Never for a while did I think of any plan of action that we as a family could have taken to get ourselves back on track. Today I will see to it that we are more united and, if not, what steps can be taken to bring all of us closer together. However, I also believe that the need of the hour is very important. I did not do so then. I was content with having meals at my relatives' homes and gossiping with them.

It was the morning of 3 May 2004 when my family and I arrived in Calcutta. Our tickets were arranged by my paternal Aunt. For my family then, every little bit of help was useful.

If my mother had not done her part then, it would not have been possible for me to receive any kind of education nor would I have met my best friend. For all this, I will always be immeasurably grateful to her. On our arrival, we were greeted very well by my maternal Uncle and his family. The first shock came when after a couple of hours my father sitting beside my mother and her brother told me to start working because he did not have money to feed me or educate me. My first expression was one of disbelief, "What was that all about?"

I was not happy with my father. For a few days I thought everyone had forgotten about it but this assumption was a mistake. I was taken to a shop in Chandni Chowk where computers and its peripherals were sold. I was told to work in the storehouse and look after the stock. Was I really up for it? I was not even sure if I could do it. With no proper clothes to wear and no good slippers to wear, initially I felt very depressed.

However, the people in the market were such that I did not feel inferior at all. My father was working at a marble dealer's place for which he travelled 15 kilometers every day. The salary he got was Rs. 3000. Our situation was pathetic. We were told by our relatives to vacate their premises and look for a rented room.

The behaviour of my relatives made me think, – how could someone who showed so much love to me previously, now speak to my family and me like this? Actually I was not aware of how this world worked. I felt horrible for my parents. I realized how they tried to keep us happy and shield us from the pain they were going through. But this time shielding us was not in their hands.

After 11 days of staying at someone's place, we shifted to a newly rented room. By using the word "someone", I am referring to my relatives with sarcasm. With a tiffin bag in tow I started travelling in local trains every day from Belur to Howrah, because I was now an employee at a computer shop. This was common in Calcutta. I was filled with doubts because I had never done anything like this before. I also felt that it was too early for me. Even if I wanted to leave the job, I could not do so. Tall buildings and people all around made me feel fearful. In Kathmandu I had never seen something like this. In the meanwhile, I started developing rotten feet. While going to work, I would open my slippers and hold them in my hands. My feet looked awful. If you fear something then that something becomes a reason for your troubles and the same happened with me. I was miserable at work.

On my way back home, I would look for a bus that was empty and sit at the extreme end. I would lower my face and start crying. I had to ensure that I cried softly, in a whisper. I did not want anyone to hear my cries.

I would cry alone to give some recourse to my emotional pain. At home, my father was not in a mood to console me at all. Where else did I have to go? Everyone backed out. The manner in which my boss scolded me made me feel miserable. All this led to me developing a sense of low self worth. Be it at home or at work, I began demeaning myself more and more.

My feet were starting to rot so I started walking barefoot. I could see my mother cry because of the simple fact that she could not get me treated. This showed how helpless we had become as a family. My work lasted for 18 days because on the eighteenth day I went to ask my boss for leave. My feet looked like stale food with fungus all over it.

It was then that I sensed my feet say something to me – they said, "Don't stop Yuvi. You might be in a bad state right now but please continue your walk of life and give it the shape you have always dreamed of. It will be tough for a while but this darkness will fade away if the flame of hope inside you is always alive.

If people label your travails silly or trivial, let them. You know best what you are dealing with and only your heart and mind understand this. Remain strong and when down fight with all your might, to rise again. Don't ever let yourself give up even when the urge to do so is strong. You might think my boss would have allowed me to take leave and go back home. But he was not very nice with me. I was constantly making mistakes at work and he would get very impatient and irritable with me. As I pleaded for one week's leave, he hurled abuses at me. I took money from my boss and left. Hurt and depressed I went back home but the sum of Rs. 500 that I had earned made me realize how much one has to do to earn money. On my way back home, I took a bus seat in the last corner where no one was sitting and I cried a lot. Infact, it was painful trying to stem my tears. It made me realize the value of my father's earnings. Prior to this I had not cared to know about how my father was earning money.

If you care even a bit for your parents, then respect the money that they spend on you. They will never say a word and do everything to make you feel on top of the world. They often try to keep us away from the harsh realities of the world and this heightens the onus on us to be sensitive to the sacrifices our parents make for us.

I had many dreams before coming to Calcutta but after seeing what the real world was like my dreams were shattered. As I write this my eyes are welling up. However, this is not making me feel weak, it's only adding fuel to my will in many dimensions. Now I only believe that had all this not happened to me then I would not have developed my inner strength. Today, if anyone even threatens to throw me down I can smile back with an unbreakable inner resolve. A person who has risen through the worst, phoenix like, is unlikely to be fazed by troubles. The worst times shape you as an individual. So, instead of posting updates on Facebook or Twitter, deal with it and continue to be sanguine. You might ask, why be cheerful? Your true character is defined while dealing with the worst. So don't brood, instead use the opportunity for self growth. Every problem is an opportunity for you to grow.

My cousin brother helped us with some cash for the treatment of my feet. Even when I was at home, I did not get the rest and recovery I needed. I did not have the luxury of a family rallying around me. Every evening I would go and fetch drinking water for our family. To fetch drinking water was like a battle because there was no bicycle or a vehicle, which could help me in bringing the water home.

I began giving importance to every single thing around me. The water I brought helped my family quench their thirst. The money I made in 18 days helped them to buy vegetables for few a days. So, with every small step I took I valued the littlest of things.

In reality I am very selfish. I don't mean to say this with a sense of pride but I've realized that life's value can only be appreciated when one values whatever one has. I learnt this fact in a very discouraging environment. What now makes sense to me is having continued to learn and striven hard in all aspects of life. Sometimes we fail to realize that people who are selfish or cruel have often become like that as a result of their life experiences. Rather than judging them unfairly or dismissing them, we should try and understand their reasons for being the way they are.

When I was made to discontinue my studies and work, I was able to break through the ice and discover that some people appearing to be cruel and cunning to others are the ones seen to be valuing every small thing in their lives and they do not tolerate the misuse of anything. This fact is something we don't want to discover because we are so preoccupied with our own thoughts and motives. If humanity exists then people would care enough to understand the underlying causes that lead people to become the way they are. I was living in a state where I was simply waiting for the days to pass by. I wanted to run faster than time and let life end. None of my relatives were by our side. Deep within I felt cheated. Someone who showed so much love to me did not even come to visit or talk to us that too when we were now so close, in physical proximity, to them. I had a growing sense of hatred towards people around me. I felt small and insignificant in a city like Calcutta. The crowd, the people around, had smiles on their faces. What I had then was Rs. 15 in my pocket to commute from home to work, a disappointed face and a depressed heart. The work I did was way below my expectations. There were days when my heart would feel so heavy that I simply couldn't help hugging my mother tight and sobbing. Women are filled with immense inner strength but the dominance of men over them overshadows the light that they radiate to the entire family. For my mother what mattered the most was my studies. Everything she did, such as paying a bribe for a forged mark sheet of class 8 or meeting influential people to get her children educated was for a selfless cause. There are no adjectives that can fully define what a mother encompasses. During the immeasurably trying times, she decided to fight like a brave soldier. She kept going with the resource of her inner strength and courage, and inspired by my mother's walk of courage, I have titled this book 'A Walk'.

Now my mother has become older yet recalling the memory of her steel during our toughest times continues to be an inspiration and enables me to face challenges with her example of calling on one's inner strength.

Going back to the story of my younger days and my mother's seminal role in helping our family and me overcoming our challenges, I'm heartened to recount that she finally succeeded in her attempts. Even now the memory overwhelms me. I started going to school once again. But there was a difference now. I was not the same as I was before. I was filled with hatred for all the rich people around and even a joke which made people laugh would have no impact on me. Teachers grew puzzled about me. Everyone around me was smiling, laughing, in short, enjoying their growing years and their school life. But for me my outlook had changed and pain had taken shape within me. I was a dull student at school. I would need the teachers to repeat themselves for me. As a result, every teacher understood that if they finish explaining something, it was important to look at me and take my confirmation that yes, the whole class had understood it.

Some people did help us but the arrogance with which they did so, was very unsettling. One particular day stands out in my memory. It was a day that I can never forget. Cricket fans go to extreme lengths sometimes to watch a match. I say this because I was such a fan who was extremely keen to see the Master Blaster Sachin Tendulkar bat. I found out that in a coffee shop a live cricket match was being shown. The people at that store seemed to be very rich. Everyone who entered seemed to have arrived in a luxury car. I was gazing through the window glass to see the match. The waiter came out towards me and told me to go home because the girls inside the coffee house were feeling uncomfortable because of my presence. I could not understand this logic at all. Whatever it was, I left the place instantly and went home. This incident was very telling, it intensified my pain because it brought home the fact of my inferior location in society – of how people now looked down on me simply because I did not have as much money as them. We are all human beings which, one would believe, connotes we have a semblance of compassion and empathy and this differentiates us from animals. Yet in practice we often seem to forget these aspects of being human and become unfeeling. We become insensitive to another's pain. We become inhuman. Having understood this I started isolating myself more. To me this world only existed for the rich and only affluence would enable my voice to be heard. My parents did not want me to see the financial difficulties they were battling so they made me stay at someone else's business address. I was marginally happier there because I was staying with someone who was one of a kind.

Studies became my biggest priority. The extent of this priority was such that I started avoiding the proposal of going home to be with my parents even for a day or two. One evening I had to go and meet them. That night was the worst in my entire life. My mother had bought some sweets and snacks while returning home from work. My father and I were waiting for my mother to come back. When she came, she was so happy to see me. I hugged her tightly as I was meeting her after a long time. While we were having dinner, a small argument began between my mother and my father. I thought it to be very normal. All of a sudden my father's strong fist hit my mother's jaw. She was badly injured and she was bleeding profusely. It changed the look of her face. How would you feel if you are made to see something that you could have never imagined in your life? What I witnessed that night left me numb with pain. Even after my father apologized for what he did, I did not sleep the whole night and felt powerless. Only if I was more grown up, it would not have happened. My mother was in severe pain even though she restrained her tears. I was in awe of my mother's inner strength. This was all just the beginning of a family conflict that was bound to occur because of the financial distress that had been looming over our family.

We keep talking of the courage of women who leave their husbands because of domestic violence. I don't call that bravery in any respect. The true bravery of a woman is manifest when she faces that situation with all her inner strength and makes it a point to always believe that this phase will pass; to keep fighting and doing her best to persevere to bring about the changes she desires.

What did my mother not do for me? Who else could have done what she did? Arranging for my fees through organizations, getting me snacks that I loved by walking a distance of about seven kilometers. For me, my mother would transform a dark night into a full moon night. I can speak endlessly about my mother. However, the fact is that each one of us who has our mother around us – we are indeed privileged. While for our mothers, we become a source of their happiness. You don't need to do much for it. You only need to make sure that you are happy. The point I am making is that the prime source of a mother's happiness is her child's happiness. One last line for all of us to embed in our heart, "Let us all be grateful to our mothers each day because mothers are truly great." This is what I realize now but then I never felt that gratitude which I feel now.

What do you really do when you are a student who has so much of a burden riding on his mind all the time? To be honest I never gave attention to the *horrible-ness* that was going on at home. Why would I?

I had a clear mind and set goals – to score well in my boards and pave the way for bringing about happiness at home. Being a real self-critic, I kept myself on my toes. If any of my relatives showed me the negative side, I would stay away from them. I was not ready to accept any negative comments. Looking at my palm, I always told myself, my destiny is in my hands and no one gets to decide what I become. I will carry this attitude to my grave.

Seriously, why should we depend on opinions that people have about us. They talk so because deep down what resides within them is disbelief. Why don't we pick ourselves up and get going with what we want to do? Motivation, to me, is all about my own desire to go out there and give it my all. Whether I win or lose I must have that feeling of satisfaction, the derivation of which is only possible if I give my best. Comparing myself with anyone else will only push me into a pit. You are unique dude, you are special. Don't believe me just because I say it with real confidence. Instead ask yourself if you're confident enough to go out there and do it for yourself.

There is no greater motivator than you yourself. Why lean on someone's shoulder. Strengthen yourself. Why wait for someone to pick you up?

It sounds harsh but this is reality, leaning on others is not worth it because people are not always dependable.

I gave my school leaving exams after which, I waited for the results. This truly was a big mistake. Knowing that my family situation was not good, I preferred staying at home and fooling around. With the passage of time, I have realized that being idle can only worsen your prospect of meeting with the right opportunity. The words irresponsible and carefree defined me in the interim between my exams and the publication of my results. I faced the consequences of this very soon. My father lost his job, and once my results came out, getting admission in high school became tough. I wanted to take up science so I went to a school and approached a school but eventually I ended up taking commerce. The event that took place between me and the school authorities was very depressing. They threw my mark sheet on my face and said. "Go get some marks added and then think of taking up science".

A screwed man does not feel bad when he is always at the receiving end. However, if the same thing happens to him at home, he is for sure hit hard from within. My father clearly told me that he couldn't pay for my higher secondary school. To top it all, the night that followed after my results were out was not sad but beyond sad. I thought my results will bring some happiness at home. It was midnight, my sleep broke and I could see my father raising his hands on my mother for some reason. I could not see this happen. For the first time in my life, I stopped his hands that were about to hit my mother again. He got furious, came running after me, and ended up hitting me with a rod because of which I carry a scar on my back till today. I walked out of home in anger. It was 1 am and I went to one of the closest grounds. I cried incessantly. Why did this happen? Why does my father beat my mother all the time? I asked myself.

Rarely do you ever get beaten by your parents when your board results are good. My attempt of saving my mother from being slapped was completely misunderstood by my father. Ever since that incident his mere presence at home would make me angry. I told my mother, on several occasions, that she should give up living with my father. I was very wrong to even say that because for a mother it is her child that is important for whom she is always willing to bear all the pain.

From then onwards even if he said a word to my mother, I would tell him to stop it there and then. I did this because I wanted things to be normal. To me my father was no more a hero who took me for bicycle rides when I was small, someone who made me eat whatever I liked and took me to most of the places he went, all the while holding my hand.

My mother wanted me to stop being mad at him. She must have said so because she understood the real cause of my father's anger. Not being able to earn and feed his family members was making him feel incapable. Today, with the passage of time I have understood the reasons which propelled him to behave that way. It is normal for anyone to react like this when they are feeling inferior about, and frustrated with, themselves.

The lesson I suppose I am still trying to not only learn but also to embed into my system is of how important it is to figure out the real cause before jumping to any conclusion. Having said that we hardly ever privilege understanding over judging.

If only I had taken up a job then, I surely would have been able to get admission into a high school. But this thought came to my mind when it was too late. I wanted to study so I started looking for schools offering higher secondary education free of cost. How foolish was I? Everyone around me only showed me the negative side and not the positive side. When things are bad, people around you make it even worse by their words. One day, when I returned home after having looked for schools, I was disheartened. A question I kept asking myself was, "Why did I even study?" When my mother came back from work, I told her to come to the ground along with me. I said so because I did not want to involve my father in all this at all. I told her about all my worries and I put my head on her lap and cried my heart out. I could not stop myself from crying. With tears rolling down my face I told my mother that I wanted to die and not live anymore because this world is only for the rich and not for people like us. She slapped me and told me to stop being a coward. "Men don't cry so stop brooding. We will see this phase through", she said.

I literally felt ashamed of myself. The next day she called me to her office and handed me Rs. 4000. She said go and take admission in Shri Jain Vidyalaya. I did not understand how my mother was able to do all this in such a short span of time.

Obviously, without wasting time I went to the school and paid the entire sum to take up a stream, which was not of my choice, that is, Commerce.

Choices we make are often shaped by the resources we possess. These resources are defined by you only that is why only if I had been a bit more prudent about my circumstances it would have enabled me to take up science and do what I wanted.

In life, whatever you want, you need to inject a fact into your system and that is, "I am the most important." You let yourself be dependent on others for something you want to accomplish and you won't get anywhere. It ought to be an all out effort coming from your end. You want it so you should be the one going all out for it. How do you do that is all up to you, isn't it? If you find that it's tough getting it, then is it something worth sacrificing for is a question for you to answer.

The reason why I say this is not because I could not do it and want people to do it for the sake of their own dreams. The mere fact that this world in reality is very harsh propels me to share my experiences and, more importantly, my learning with you.

The very first day of school, I was late. There was this teacher who made me stand outside the gate and said, "What kind of school dress is that?" Anyone would have said that. I was wearing a white shirt with a torn collar and slippers instead of school shoes. Why was I dressed such? Dear Sir, because I could not afford a proper uniform. The teacher however did not understand. He made me feel ashamed of myself. Dejected and disheartened, I returned home without attending a single class. My father was unperturbed to see me back from school so early, but my mother came up to me and enquired. I took off my bag and with tears rolling down my cheeks asked her why would a school let a poor student like me study? I don't even have the clothes and shoes to be one amongst them.

She hugged me tight and made me sit beside her. My tears did not stop even then. When you're made to feel so hopeless and poor, who would not have tears? My mother was the only one who knew me inside out. Even today, she gets to know when I am upset or I am happy without me having to even call her up. That's something magical and beautiful. The only guidance I received from her is this, "If you have to win in life then you need to know how to face criticism. Today your teacher insulted you, do something in future that he is compelled to admire you as his student." So I guess most of you have understood from where these thoughts of mine emanate. I then rejoined school four days after my mother bought me a shirt and a pair of shoes. She told me to give my best to my studies and never complain about anything I did not have. At school there were all intelligent guys with me. I found myself to be a very poor student in terms of the kind of knowledge they already had about commerce and its sub topics.

Teachers gave attention to only those students taking private tuitions from them. In class they presumed that all of us knew everything. Apart from a few teachers I found all of them to be the same. I was worried about the fact that if I don't join tuition classes, I will fail in the exams. The only alternative left for me was to read as much as I could in the library and practice accounts. I took four months to understand journal entries. I found accounts tough. The only subject that excited me was economics. some of the students had a sense of arrogance only because of the tuitions they took which helped them score well in their exams.

I was all alone so I decided to move to the last bench in the class beside a boy who seemed to be very engrossed in his studies. He was the first friend I made in two years. One day, our economics professor asked the boy a question. He was lean and thin. His face became red because he was very nervous. Someone sitting beside him told the teacher he was unable to speak in English. The whole class started laughing, I felt bad for him.

Why do we think ourselves to be so learned when we cannot even show courtesy to others? Once the class got over, Pankaj and I went to him and shook hands. We asked him to join us in the last bench. Initially he was hesitant but after a few days he started sitting with us.

When did I last laugh, maybe some years back when I was in Kathmandu? These two guys were devoted, passionate about studies and nothing seemed to deter their spirits but at the same time they were funny and made me laugh all the time. For a while, even I would forget my miserable life.

I will share this secret with all of you. During break time, that is at 8 am, I would go downstairs near the canteen and get myself a dosa to eat. I would eat first and because it used to be so crowded, I would not pay at all and go back to class. I did this not once but on several occasions. After all, when you want to eat something you like, you don't know what ethical or unethical is, you just do it. I would also be wary of my friends and pray that they don't come downstairs while I was eating because I did not want to share my food with them. I was mean, mean for something I wanted to eat all alone.

I had this side of me too. I have not forgotten those days when I would walk 15 kms only to save a bus fare of Rs. 6. Saving it meant a lot to me as I used it to eat two samosas and an ice cream.

I started witnessing the shift in my mindset. From a carefree guy who did not know the value of money, I was now willing to go a mile to save a rupee.

You must be thinking of my life as supremely tough. But to surprise you all I was enjoying it now. It became a part of my daily routine. You don't cry in pain for a wound you know will not heal at all. It was the same for me now.

So when my father lost his job, I took up a job at a friend's shop. It was very near to school. After my school got over at 10 am, I would go to his shop and start working. Cleaning the shop and fetching drinking water were all a part of my responsibilities. My friend's mother came to the shop and told me to start selling hangers. I tried but I was not vocal like other sellers. So again, things got bad and my belief about rich people being cruel intensified. At home everyone was furious with me because I was working. I was no more ashamed of what they had to say. I understood that to earn your bread and butter, you need to slog.

Go out there and do it. Even if the work is of a low stature, doing it should not make you feel ashamed because the money you earn helps you feed your family and if you are really bothered about what people will say then do one thing – go to their home and ask for food. They will not hesitate to shut the door on your face.

I refused to do so now. I was very much aware of who was what to me. Sweet words of anyone made no sense to me. Somewhere then I did not even feel I was living. This continued for 12 days because my health started deteriorating. Final exams were drawing near too. Gosh!!! I had to quit but quitting without money was not possible because my family needed money. The amount did not matter. When you don't have a single penny even a rupee that you get from someone is like a million rupees. Rs. 500 that I got from my friend who was running the shop meant a lot to me. I was going back home with a sense of pride that finally I had grown up.

I reached home to find nobody and I was famished so I went into the kitchen to see if there was something to eat. I checked every possible food container but there was nothing to eat, not even a grain of rice. I went into the room, threw my school bag aside and fell onto the bed. It was more than painful. Yet again, I had tears rolling down my cheeks. When my father and Jitu came home, I did not complain that there was nothing to eat. Instead, I took out the money I had and gave him Rs. 400, telling him that you might consider me to be the worst son in the world but I will always do every bit I can for my family. For the rest of the night, I was thinking of how my life was and why was I heading that way?

Money can be immaterial in a sense but it has its own value, which can never be ignored. People who think of adding value in other peoples' lives are in a state where they think of money as inconsequential because they are content with what they have or have achieved some level of financial security in their lives. In case you are financially troubled, then you don't think of making peoples' lives better instead you think of ways to fix your financial mess.

In life, many amongst us face trying situations of different kinds, it really is not easy, it breaks us down, it makes us weak and as a result we fall into depression.

Don't expect me to give you a remedy for your depression. You call it depression, just have some courage and look around at home. See your mother, see your father, they toil hard day and night so that you, yes you, do well in life. On the contrary, what you do is ruin their expectations. And hello, even when you do this, they don't get depressed. They fight it out, they remain determined to build you again and that is why they forgive you.

If you see things not going your way, cry your heart out and once you are done with the crying find the resolve deep within to overcome your situation. In spite of all this don't forget to be compassionate. If you lose compassion then you will not help yourself grow as a human being.

I understood the situation then and acted upon it. I could have decided to wait and watch and see what my parents do about it. Had I done that, we four would not have had dinner that night and maybe not even had breakfast the next morning.

My feet are a metaphor that distill all my learnings – that they should continue to walk – come what may. If I let them rest, I would be committing a grave mistake. It was only because I decided to walk from school to my friend's shop was I able to make some money for the sake of my family. Even in other cases, if you don't walk then how do you ever achieve what you want to or how do you figure out what you want to become?

Initially I was looking for ways for my father or my mother to help me out but after this incident, I decided to take matters into my own hands and fight against the harsh realities we were facing.

I think taking an initiative to fight back and win over your difficult situation is the key. So are we fighting back or resorting to dependency?

My mother had tears in her eyes that night when she saw me. She could never think that her son was becoming responsible so fast. Only she mattered to me then and even the slightest pain in her eyes made me impatient.

I had made up my mind, to live my life for the sake of my family. Exams were coming closer and I was studying literature in the morning and my father called me to help him with some work in the kitchen. I did not reply.

Filled with anger he came to me and shouted. I was not fond of his presence at home. So I told him to keep quite as I was studying. In anger he snatched my book and tore it into two and then he threw it into the drain. I got my book out of the drain and told him about the arrival of a day when books like this would bring forth my real potential that was lying somewhere deep within me.

It discourages a son when his father does something like this but if you have a strong inner belief of being able to accomplish all that you want from life, a situation like this won't discourage you. It will deepen your determination to accomplish your goals. That's why I always say, "It is my belief that is important, not anybody else's".

How do I describe my life? Adjectives fall short when I try to define it. There were times when it seemed pleasant and times when I felt as if my existence was worthless. At times, it I felt I wanted to sort differences with my father and on certain occasions I would think of his death. Yes, I thought of all this about him.

When things like this keep happening in life, you want to get into bed and go off to sleep, believing that sleep for an hour or two will help you overcome some level of pain.

My father was not a pain for me, it was his behavior and ways in which he tortured my mother mentally and physically that made me anti my father. All this while, I used to seek a time when we as a family would come together and stay united in both happiness and sorrow.

If I am to admit something, then it has to be my arrogance towards my father and people around me. I was filled with hatred for everyone I met. Maybe I found the world to be very rude and harsh. Was I doing anything wrong? Yes, I was. I could have fostered myself to be compassionate even with such trying circumstances. If only was I able to do it, I would have developed myself not only as a strong individual but as a man of courage, a man of compassion and a man who never gives up.

If you are going through something similar, please don't get influenced by this temporary wind to start hating people all around. Let us always believe that nothing apart from our own happiness is permanent. I was blown away by the wind that was blowing around me every now and then. What I forgot was the fact that I was unique and every difficult situation in life comes to see the strength that lies within you. If you're strong then you will not give in, come what may.

I just forgot how lovely my father was. I forgot the magic he would do to get me what I wanted. To me then my father was simply a man whom I hated because he was venting his frustration on my family and me. Who does not express his frustration and why would someone not express it in front of someone he loves the most. I hate myself for never being able to understand these facts then.

After a while he left us and went to New Delhi because of a decent job offer he got, for which he did not have to incur any expense for himself and could send money back home.

The devil inside me was so happy when I saw him go. My mother and Jitu were not happy about this at all. Studying in class 12, I had to make it count this time. I was convinced of this fact because I had nothing to lose and everything to gain. With this intent at heart I devoted myself with utmost sincerity and passion towards my studies. Then getting into a premier college was a big deal. Pankaj, Siddharth and I started working with immense dedication. We paid no attention to the lectures and started studying on our own.

Each one of us was competing against each other but it was only to polish our own knowledge and have an in-depth understanding of whatever we studied. Apart from studies we also had fun when we watched porn videos at Pankaj's place. I had given up my home to only be with these two friends, because being with them was how I would keep up with the intensity that was needed to overcome my situation.

We joined a coaching class for accounts and the teacher teaching was more than remarkable. He not only taught us, but rather, he made us live accounts. It would all begin at 6:30 pm and go on till 8 pm. Sometimes, he would ask us to stretch and complete the sum and only then proceed towards our respective homes. Ask him a silly question and he would make sure even that was answered. Seeing him explain different chapters of accounts and sums involved in each of them made me feel dedication backed with sincerity can define the real purpose of life.

There is so much to be learnt from people around us. We really don't need a person to come and rescue us from our problems. What we truly need is to realize the importance of learning from people we encounter.

Having said so, I myself was not able to appreciate my father. Working on my self development was the need of the hour. However, at the time this never came to mind. Like a person seeking to reach his destination, I was so occupied with the thought of doing my best in my school leaving exams that nothing else made sense to me then. This habit is indeed a drawback in itself. Although you might achieve your goals, but the ignorance towards others will haunt you someday for sure. People around us are important. Never should we commit the mistake of undermining or ignoring them thinking that they don't mean anything to us.

Meanwhile, my friendship with Pankaj and Siddharth had reached its next level. If one of us felt like giving up, the other would lift his mood and get us back to working together and help us move towards our goal. Pankaj's home had become the centre point for us. We would assemble there with all our books and begin doing what we were meant to do.

His grandpa would be with us too. He was old and seriously unwell but when it came to scolding us, he would make us feel stupid. Siddharth regularly got thrashed by him.

Old people at home are like gold. They add a charm to the atmosphere in the house and make things lighter. I often wonder about the beauty an old age home is blessed with. Why do young people like us give up on the beautiful wealth of having elderly parents with them? One smile from an elderly person brightens my day. To me it is like a soul that pours down its entire being into only blessing me. As youngsters, let us be more caring towards the elderly, because not only will they feel good but we too will find a reason to continue persevering. ☺

On the other side, my mother started worrying because of my absence from home and she spoke about it with my father over the phone. I got a call from him and he said, "Which girl are you fucking around with?" My response was simple and straight, "When my results come, you will know which girl I was fucking around with." After saying this, I felt sad and depressed but not for long.

At times, my mother would not have enough money to let me go to Pankaj's place. This made me develop plan B which was to fool the ticket inspector and move out of Howrah station. The only way to be able to do that was to walk with confidence, and for that I would pull my sleeves up and walk slowly with my head held up high. I would intentionally go closer to the Ticket Inspector at Howrah Station and once I crossed his zone it was like, "*Aaaj toh bach gaye bhai*"(I got saved!)

This way of mine was because the only money I would have would be Rs. 15, which was inadequate. My mother would only give me this much money. After reaching Howrah I would walk down about 4 kms to reach Pankaj's place. When it was time to return home at 8 pm, I would use the rush at the station to escape the Ticket Checkers. I love eating snacks so I would buy some snacks for Rs. 5 and the rest then was enough to get myself a cold drink. This was a typical day for me.

Just like you polish a tarnished mirror to make it shine, the same applied to me. With each passing day, I bettered my grasp over accountancy. Some energies around were supporting me in a big way. On the other hand I was becoming more arrogant. I would deny work my mother would delegate me.

Jitu would come to me for help in his studies. I would rudely tell him to do his work himself. Better at studies but bad at home, this was not what I wanted but I could not help it then because I only wanted to do one thing and that was to get into the most prestigious college in India. This was not only to get a good education from the best college but to show some of my relatives that I was not just anybody. I was somebody. When one of my relatives threw my accounts book saying that you will never be able to get into any good college, it hurt me very much. Deep inside, I became determined to do everything it takes to prove him wrong.

I was eager to prove myself to people who shoved me aside, ridiculed me that I was incapable to accomplish anything significant. How could they? This question made me sense the necessity to achieve despite all odds.

At the same time, I wished to have someone who understood me and gave me a shoulder I could lean on. This was never to happen because none of them understood what was going on in my heart. Yes, to put myself back after depressing moments and to start afresh was my sole objective. The pond near my house helped me a lot. I would sit there for hours in the evening, shout and release the sorrow and grief within me. This was the only recourse I had because the rest of the world apart from my two great friends had abandoned me.

Wiping tears from my eyes was actually a recharging process so that I could get on with that one single goal I wanted to achieve. I needed my full self so I could give it my best shot.

One day when we had our accounts lecture going on, the professor came with a bundle of mark sheets which contained marks that we scored in the pre-board accounts exam.

He called out everyone's name and handed over their mark sheets to them. I was the last one to receive mine. I was shocked seeing my marks and felt like punching the professor. He had cut my marks on useless grounds. I was furious so when he made me stand up and give me a justification for scoring low marks, I said, "In the boards I'll score the highest". Everyone turned their heads around to look at me. "Let them see me", these were the exact words I told myself then.

My coaching professor once commented about me and shared it with the rest of the students in his coaching class. He said, "Yuvraj can't be a Sachin Tendulkar because he is not born with the talent. He is Rahul Dravid who will keep working until he has mastered that talent." I did not get overwhelmed by his words then because to a guy like me whose life itself was so upside down, the compliment seemed unworthy.

We were also taking tuitions for statistics and as the board exams drew nearer we three friends decided to start practicing statistics from the beginning and do as many sums as possible and practice accounts questions which were set by our accounts teacher.

Racking our brains to solve such difficult questions was an uphill task for us but it was fun too. In the middle of the night, even in my sleep I would talk about an adjustment entry that was possible for final accounts.

We three friends enjoyed studying together. Besides studying, we would talk non veg stuff amongst ourselves and make sure that we were in really high spirits. When we did not have the solution to a problem, we would call up JC Sir at anytime. If he was unavailable then we would scratch our heads and move out to eat something.

This whole experience will always be memorable to me. We three friends are in different fields, cities and jobs but when we meet, we start talking about those days.

It is important for us to have a passion for, and enthusiasm towards, achieving our goals. We should be able to walk that extra mile even if it takes a bit of our life from us. I firmly believe in the theory of giving it all and enjoying it at the same time. The most important thing that happens is you don't waste your time roaming around aimlessly with friends in places like malls, restaurants or in a park with your girlfriend. Do these things even add value to your life? Yes, they do at times but mostly they don't.

If I let this life go aimlessly then why am I even living it, or if I am living it why do I have eyes, ears, hands and legs? Are they to only help you to go with the flow or to make your own destiny? To me, depression which people talk about all the time, is not a disease but it is a sign of the negative attitude we have let develop within us, the basis of which is temporary. Even if we have failed in many attempts, the process makes us better than we were before. Even if we have had failed relationships we have a lot in life to explore. Even if we are handicapped, we have new ways to innovate and do things differently. All of this would have been easy to understand only if we were men and women filled with gratitude.

Then, I did not realize this and that's why irrespective of how I was doing amongst my friends, I was still not a good son. Buddy, we sadly realize our mistakes when that moment is gone but it's never late to start developing this within ourselves so that we don't do it ever again. We all are great and unique people with great potential. Let us work hard, be strong and gracious for all this life has to offer and set an example for others around us. This will surely bring harmony and hope to a society governed by all kinds of anxieties and greed.

I am writing right now mainly to be able to communicate to the readers of this book about living life to create value. This value in no way can be driven by self-centric emotions. It has to arise out of our sense of compassion, only then can the value we decide to create last long and not get blown away like the sand that gets blown away when the wind comes.

Which man does not want a girl who loves him? At the end of the day, once done with all our studying what we gossiped about was having a girlfriend. We spoke about this in a very rough fashion but honestly, we never had intentions of doing what we spoke about. To simplify it, our gossip about girls and our actions towards women were in no way correlated.

Time was passing by and we were like pioneers of accountancy, adjustment entries were on our finger tips.

I was more than confident about my command over the subject. Two weeks were left for our exams and I was willing to work harder. The passion intensified with every single passing day. If my mother or anybody spoke negatively about what I intended to achieve, they would not have to even wait for a second and I would respond angrily. If negativity was matter, I would pick it up and thrash it all the way round. Physically anyone might beat you but mentally it is next to impossible to get beaten if you have developed your mental strength. Thanks to everything that happened previously, I was eager to change my destiny on my own. We three friends were of the same mind. We were like many-in-body-one-in-mind.

Pankaj's grandpa passed away a week before our exams. I was very saddened because now no one would scold me like he did. No one would query me about my origin and my parents every single time I went to his place. Grand pa loved Pankaj a lot. So, Siddharth and I thought of going together to meet him. When I saw him, I was amazed to see the kind of spirit he showed through his calm and collective behavior. He took hold of his own emotions and was determined to get the incomplete task done. How did he do that? He was still smiling along with us.

There are times when we set out to be an inspiration for others but at times there are people, touching your soul not by their words but through their actions.

I was amongst those who after a point give up, Siddharth was not one of them. He would sit with a question until he had solved it even if it took him the entire day. For me, his determination was an inspiration. I realized that although I might not be able to solve a problem right now but if there is a sincere determination to solve it, then you will be able to solve it. To be honest, I have learnt more from people like him than from my own life.

It is not possible to achieve your goals or make a future for yourself without someone's help. Help in this case does not mean dependence but it means of time when others move you to push yourself harder and if you've been doing that already then to push yourself harder still. Even today, there are times when I feel my existence is useless. It does happen. You can't help it. We are humans with emotions that keep fluctuating. A moment comes where I see someone walking by or someone at a shop, or a laborer working really hard to only be able to feed his family. Feeding his family is his goal and for that he is giving it his all.

So, when I have a dream to achieve, a purpose of life to fulfill then why can't I fight back? Who in this world other than me knows me best? I shed some tears when I am alone for a while, and then I start all over again. Doing this to myself on a regular basis has helped me shape my life and so will be the case if you do something similar but you never give up. That's the biggest disease around and no medicine other than your will to fight back can cure it.

We decided that we would be studying together at Siddharth's place for the duration of the exams. I told my mother about it. She was not happy but I had to do it. She very well knew of what I was up to so she did not hesitate for long. We started with Hindi, which was again a big pain for us. None of us were sure how we would study a subject like this. When nothing was going into our brains, we decided to mug it up.

There are times when we look for ways to do a particular thing and when all our tried and tested ways fail to bring the desired result we give up. Even then you must find a way of getting it done. Don't stop until you have accomplished what you set out to achieve. Stopping, thinking that there is no way onwards from here is simply a sign of giving up on your belief of being able to get it done.

Our passion, commitment and sincerity were always extant. We three friends did not want ourselves to be meager people. We wanted to do our best. Every single exam that we appeared for, we told ourselves of giving it our best shot. We did not sleep for seven days. We were awake all the time. If we felt sleepy we would watch *Fashion TV*.

Doing this made us feel a bit lighter and recharged us. What more? We also watched porn movies to destress. We would study through the night and once we would realize it was daybreak we would rush back to the study room, revise once again and make sure we completed the entire syllabus by 8 am. Once done, we would head to the exam hall and give our best. I must admit I never felt stressed or tired then and this seemed miraculous. They say that when you are fighting for your dreams, stress and tiredness take a back seat.

Once I was done with my exams, I went home, slept early and woke up very late. My mother was kind enough to not wake me up. Even when I did not speak a word, she would herself figure out what I really needed and do things accordingly. Women, in my view, are truly great. I wholeheartedly admit they are superior to men when it comes to being patient, diligent and witty. Sadly, their attributes are never rewarded by us. When I get married, I vow to appreciate my wife and enable the best for my family and myself. We three sincere creatures now thought of having some fun. I was able to convince my mother to give me some money so that I could go out for a movie with my friends. After nine years, I went to a movie theatre and then we had some street food. The feeling was great. Calcutta is known for its street food, the taste of which can never be the same elsewhere.

I was not a fun loving person and even if I was, I always hesitated when it came to taking the initiative. So, my friends loved playing pranks on me and pulled my leg very often. I would feel bad but could not help how I was.

After a few days, we had to start preparing for the CPT exams in order to pursue Chartered Accountancy. While both my friends were devoted to start studying again, I wasn't. I started ignoring the importance of the CA exams.

Even if it does not matter to me today, I have learnt the hard way about ignorance. The learning was, if I become ignorant towards my pursuance then even life would become ignorant of my wishes and throw me down.

The other bad thing about me was that I would never listen to anyone. It was mainly because I had been amongst people who only imparted negative views which my heart was not willing to accept. What I only cared for was my heart and whether it made me feel like doing something about it or not. I did it or else, would throw the words from others right out of both my ears. This was not good. I was so self centered because of which I thought that people around me did not have any problems to deal with. I missed out on being compassionate.

Even today I am working upon this trait of mine and am confident of being able to get over it sooner or later.

You can't stop at a point and say that you have reached your destination. Actually, that point should be a starting point for us. Nelson Mandela once quoted, "After climbing a great hill, one only finds that there are many more hills to climb".

When my results came out, it was an unforgettable moment of joy for me, I scored the best marks of my entire academic life. My friends and I were overjoyed. I was told by my mother to tell my father about this. With an inner desire to embarrass him, I called him up and told him about my marks. He was in tears. I never knew my father could be so emotional. I was startled. He said, "Beta, mujhe pata hai ki tu mujhse kitna nafrat karta hai magar teri iss jeet mein sabse jyada khus tera baap huaa hai" (My son I know how much you hate me but in this victory of yours the person who is happiest for you is your father).

Was that for real? I could not believe my ears. How could a father like him who always fought with me, and beat me whenever he was angry utter such words?

Actually, we humans possess both good and bad. It is all within us. The underlying cause of someone's outrageous actions is never given the focus it truly deserves. Even after this, we call ourselves humans. Sad, but that's the truth.

If I am questioned on how would I have dealt with my father then I would say that I should have tried harder to make things better between him and me. Certainly, because it would require so much effort from me I would become a hero that way. I never did anything like that, so I never became a hero in that episode of my life.

With respect to that phase of my life, I ended up becoming a coward. However, with the passage of time, I have learnt to become a hero. Every single time things hit me or someone hurts me, I try to become a hero. Not by punching that person but by acting on ways to certainly make things better between him and me. I continue to do that and hope to master this very art perfectly in days to come. Glory lies in making peace.

When I returned home, now all my relatives were calling my mother and congratulating her on my results. I felt bad to see people calling us up when things were going well and knowing that when we were helpless and were in need of help they shunned us.

At the end of the day, I am thankful to my feet that kept moving and never gave up. It was this walk that motivated me to push myself to achieve something phenomenal in my scheme of things. This walk brought my way friends filled with passion and the sincerity to work hard. Had I discontinued this walk, my schoolteacher would have been proven right by sending a student with a torn school shirt and plastic shoes back home. I felt the importance of walking every time I saw my feet that never let me stop and made me move every moment.

Shocks are what I am used to and dealing with them comes more easily to me now. The tough situations that have come my way have helped me develop inner strength. And today my tears have dried up and my tendency to react anxiously has been substituted by a great level of calmness.

There was a time when it was all tough. Easy ways were hard to come by. I certainly wished things to be simpler but they never were and that is why today I take everything with a great deal of seriousness and maturity. Irrespective of all this, my craziness is still alive.

After our results were published, it was time to apply for the college we dreamt of studying in. Once the list of shortlisted students came out, it brought me nothing but anxiety. I can't forget that night when I cried and did not sleep.

Getting into St. Xaviers was my dream and I had given it my all. I started standing in front of the college from morning to evening to seek an opportunity to meet the Principal.

Watchmen were instructed to not let anybody in. Guardians of parents were standing, wanting to seek the same opportunity I was longing for. I would return home with a face that looked very sad and numb. I was cursing myself for having studied so hard. Why? Why did I fight all odds and do well in the exams if I was not going to be in the college I dreamt of. Often my mother and my father would tell me to feel good about the fact that I scored well and that, that in itself is an achievement. I did not want their consoling words then. I was adamant and would speak erratically to them. I would slap myself and punch my hand at the wall in frustration.

Taking a letter which contained details of various institutions and NGOs which were responsible for funding my education during class 10 and higher secondary studies was one way through which I could meet the principal and convince him to give me a place in my dream college.

I was not faking anymore then because all the matter in it was genuine and I had myself met people at educational institutions and NGOs to seek financial help with my studies. To my surprise even after having read my letter the principal threw it back at me.

Furious at myself, I came out of the room in anger and wanted to thrash parents who were there with a suitcase which surely must have contained a lot of cash. The power of money was such that when these people entered the room, discussions between them and the Principal went on for more than half an hour.

How is this world? I was always taught about how honesty and sincerity were the prime attributes needed in a person. Seeing all this, I could not do anything but take out all my frustration on my mother. I should not have done that. Even after venting my frustration at her, she would try and make me feel better and calm me down.

Treat your mother with a lot of respect and love, she is the person who untiringly enables and encourages you. How in the world can you even for a second ignore her well being? She never did that to you so why should you do that to her? Your wife might die and you might remarry but your mother once gone will never come back. She is precious, so treat her well and always do things that bring a smile on her face.

People around me gave me the moniker of being a mad person. Everyone said to me that it is only money or high levels of IQ which help to get a place in esteemed colleges. I was so discouraged that I began neglecting myself and developed bad eating habits. My mother was always full of praise for me but it did not matter to me much because the gravity of wanting to get into St. Xavier's blinded everything else.

I left no stone unturned. I went to church to see if the father there could help me. I even asked my father's permission to convert to Christianity. I finally made it in the third list. I compromised my CPT exams of CA and as a result I flunked and did not ever appear for the CA Exams.

On the day of admission my mother was overwhelmed to see the infrastructure of the college and kept on talking about it with our neighbors. My father made all the monetary arrangements beforehand. I was finally living my dream. Something my soul craved sincerely for a year and a half was now coming true.

Every effort put was now a source of immeasurable joy. From then onwards, I became a true believer that single minded hard work was key to unlocking the path to your dreams.

There are occasions when we feel we have missed out on the goal we had set for ourselves. This to me is a myopic way of defining our goals. I say this because even if you achieve your goals, there is something more challenging ahead of you and you need to again set a new goal for the way ahead. So what we end up doing is chasing rather than defining our life through the goals we set.

I made the mistake of defining goals with short term perspectives in mind. I soon realized, now that I was here, what now? What is my next goal?

On my first day in college I was looking around the college and wondering if it was all happening for real. This feeling continued for quite some time, which turned out to be not without caveats for me.

Most of the students I was with were rich, filthy rich according to my standards. Money had always played a cruel game in my life and even in college I saw students who would spend their parents' money lavishly. During such times I only compared myself with them and deep within felt highly inferior about myself.

Waking up in the morning at 4:30 am and leaving for college by 5 am so that I reached college by 6 am used to be tough for me. During lectures, I would look around at other students because I saw myself as the odd one out.

During break time I would either go to a tea shop where I would spend time with some of the guys with whom I believed I would be able to develop a friendship. I tried avoiding the group of students with all kinds of amenities like smart phones, cars and a lavish lifestyle.

I realized the importance of focusing on gaining more knowledge. I would spend three to four hours a day reading newspapers and magazines. This way I developed a knack to improve my vocabulary. In the library, I saw some really beautiful girls. Till now I had never thought of being with a girl but the topic of a girlfriend was so popular in college that I too wanted to have a girlfriend.

All this while, seeing the tough side of life was what I was accustomed to. So, I started engaging myself in various extra-curricular activities. I wanted to learn more about business through practical experience but the way in which our course was designed did not sound practical at all. Like school, here too we had to study, make sure that our attendance was reasonable enough to be eligible to sit for the semester exams.

Meanwhile, I became friends with a girl. To be honest she was the first girl in India who became a friend of mine. She had a husky voice, a lovely smile and her hair was luscious. I still remember the day when we both were sitting opposite each other. She was tired so she fell asleep. I was only looking at her. I did not want to take my eyes off her because all this while I had witnessed only pain and sorrowful moments. Why would I let a moment like this slip by?

Suddenly, I sneezed so loudly that she abruptly woke up. Now that she was awake, she went for her classes. Not to forget, it was only because I wanted to spend some time with her that I did not go back home and stayed at college even after my classes got over at 10 am. I stayed back because her classes started at 4 pm.

Everything around me that happened became a source of joy to me. How can I forget that day when an unknown girl offered me a chocolate bite? She happened to be from the mathematics department. Thanks to her I was introduced to a bunch of students who were really amazing. One of them is an angel to me.

All this I was getting into was in a true sense a temporary world of illusion. I started ignoring my studies. I roamed around with people uselessly. All of this was only to make more friends. It was for this reason that I performed very poorly during my first semester. Angel was amazing. She had a beautiful mind and a beautiful heart. I loved being around her.

I did not pay much heed to my poor performance. Instead, I decided to propose to the husky voiced, lovely smiled and curly haired girl. I had seen in the movies guys getting slapped when proposing to a girl. I too had the same feeling. I wanted to prove to myself that I was brave.

So after all my clues were not being understood by her, I took her to the canteen and sat opposite her so that I could not only propose but also admire her beautiful smile.

Adjectives fall short when I define what she was to me. For sure, she did hold my hand for a few minutes but after that, it was all gone. My seeking of true love did not end there. It went on and after some hook ups and short lived relationships it became pretty clear that more work was to be done on myself. By this I mean to highlight the fact that love should never be the central focus of our lives.

This is all that I know about it because in love I was always proven to be a stupid fool. To truly understand love you can resort to a book that focuses entirely upon two couples who are busy between themselves and hence forget to explore the rest of life and opportunities this life has to offer. Only thing about love is to love but never seek it back in return. A mother's love is one such example.

There is more than one side to me. One side of me wanted to rid myself of all the problems in life and make things better for not only myself but also for others. Why was it so?

While enduring this walk, what I saw were other people who were so deprived of the basic amenities of life but somehow with that little hope they had, I could see them smile. It is not easy to do so during times of hardship but such people are worth learning from. I decided to spread more smiles among such people. Superficially, people talk a lot about it and NGO'S do things but usually, in practice, all this boils down to helping rich people evade taxes.

There was this small girl who would roam around our college gate. Her mother would pick up waste from the road and find eatables from it. Her father was a drunkard so we would see him lying on the roadside unconscious.

We called her Chutki. With a lovely smile and a dimple on her cheek she was adored by most of us in college. One day, when I was buying a cigarette from a shop near our college she came up to me and wanted me to buy biscuits for her. When I bought a packet of biscuits for her, she took three biscuits out and said, "Thank you". I was startled and a bit annoyed at her. But what she did with those three biscuits was actually an inspiration for me. She went to her mother and gave her two of them and then herself ate one.

She was so small yet she had such love for her mother. Even when you are poor the selflessness with which you commit yourself towards your family needs is indeed inspirational. So, how many of us really do something like this?

When the second semester started my father was back from Delhi to be with us permanently and I was not happy about him coming home. For a year I was living peacefully with my mother and brother but now my father was coming back? I told my mother about this for which I received two tight slaps.

He came back home but from the moment he arrived I stayed away from him. I could not tolerate his presence but my mother and my brother were very happy to see him back. It was because of my hatred for him, that we two fought at home many times. I got punched on my face too for not obeying him. He started taunting me, saying that I was living on his money and showing off.

How could he? Just to prove him wrong, I took up a job in a call center right away. None at home were happy about my decision then. My mother spoke to me about this several times but I did not want to hear anything.

So, now my schedule was tight. No time for socializing, no time for family or myself. I would leave for college early morning, that is at 4:45 am, attend lectures till 10 am, spend a few hours in the college library and then go to work. With headphones on and targets on my mind, I had to make sure I exceeded my target levels. I wanted to show my father how capable I was.

I found myself alone now. I hardly had friends in college and at home, in spite of the good sum of money I earned, nobody really appreciated me.

However, my work at office was being appreciated by everyone. They felt that my accent was unique and I could do wonders with the kind of voice quality, I had. This was the phase where I learnt, worked hard and also lost myself in hedonistic pursuits.

Pleasure in the form of drinking, smoking and at times even doping with colleagues had become a part of life. For me office was slowly becoming my home. I did not like returning home after work.

There came the time when I drew the highest salary of mine till then, that was, Rs. 15000. It was summer then and my mother would have trouble storing vegetables and fruits. So I decided to buy her a refrigerator. I made the payment the very next morning and got a refrigerator for her. Even now when I go back home during holidays, I see the fridge and feel nostalgic about the bit by bit struggle that went behind affording it for my mother.

With around Rs. 2500 left now I had to run my expenses for a month. I knew how to do that. This was what I had learnt during my tough times. Tough times teach you things which best times can never do. So, instead of searching for ways to escape a tough scenario you come across you must confront it. Doing that does not take anything away from you instead it makes you explore your uniqueness which is possessed by you and only you.

Why do I cherish those days when the walk of life was extremely painful and heartbreaking? The trying times made me grow as a human being. So, if you read this book and don't learn to cherish the pain and sorrows this life of yours has to offer I will surely be disappointed.

When I would awake at 4:30 am for college, everyone at home would be asleep and even when I came back at 11:30 pm after college and work, they would be sleeping. Even if I was eager to rid my family of their financial problems, I was losing out on the togetherness between us. My eyes were always sleepy. Even during lectures in college, the professor would ask me to leave the class but would make sure that I was given attendance.

The way I hated myself can't be explained. I wanted to be the best both at work and in college. Sadly, I was not good at both. However, I continued with this life for a year or so. The reason to continue to walk then was driven by hope. I kept criticizing myself, followed by tapping myself and moving forward. Even though I did not ever say it I always felt that things will change soon.

Today, things are different with me but even then before I go off to sleep I make a virtual report in my mind of the work I accomplished throughout the day or of something new I did or learnt that day. In cases where the reports were not pleasant, I would make sure the next day I valued time more and accomplished one new thing.

You might not realize this now but this is the surest way to develop yourself. You need to be strict with yourself but compassionate to others around you.

I did not learn this lesson then. I wanted to have fun, roam around with beautiful girls, drink and party. All of this was important to me although these things did not add any meaning and value to my life.

What we all should be able to understand is the necessity to define the value we are looking to create through whatever we do. If we are able to define the value that we are looking to create then we don't get deluded from what we need to do and what we need to avoid. However, do this bearing in mind that the value defined should not be a narrow one which only sums up to you. Instead, it should encompass society or at least touch the lives of some people around you.

This helps you in not only working for your goals but also in shoring up the depleting levels of compassion in our society today.

Nobody was eager to sit with me and speak to me even for a minute in college. I was forcing myself on them. It was not appropriate but like most of us I too wanted to be with other students and have fun.

Sadly that never happened. Even at home I was treated like an outsider. This led me to take up smoking and drinking. I also got into a relationship with a girl who wanted nothing besides physical pleasure. College was about to get over and I had some recovery work to do. Unfortunately I got typhoid and the money I earned for the month of September went towards my treatment.

While I was in the process of recuperating, I met a guy in college who is my best friend today. He spoke to me about Nichiren Buddhism and how people transformed their karmas and brought happiness in their lives through this philosophy. I was overwhelmed by his words and decided to give it a try. So, every day I chanted Nam-Myoho-Renge-Kyo for five minutes with the sole purpose of being able to give my semester exams. My back was weak and I could not sit for long, also I was not aware of the syllabus.

Through chanting I found the spirit to fight back and sit for four hours in the exam and eventually clear the semester with a decent score.

The next day after the results were out, I walked up to Pranam who had told me about the law and thanked him. Our friendship started from that very day. I started practicing this wonderful philosophy with assiduous belief and faith.

I had to quit my job after sometime for health reasons. Also, my so called girlfriend went away from my life making me realize the opportunities that were ahead of me. I did not have any grudges or hatred towards her. What I had and still have is a great deal of sympathy for someone like her.

Friendship can never be defined or described and that is its beauty. You don't need to communicate to someone saying, "We are friends". It happens on its own. While college was now coming to an end some wonderful moments made those last few days memorable. However, I can't forget the last day of college for two reasons – one good and one bad. One of the professors, bearing in mind, the closeness I had developed with Pranam *(My Lajjo!)* declared us "the best couple of the B.Com (Bachelor of Commerce) morning department". The whole class burst out laughing. Pranam and I looked at each other and smiled as if we truly were one.

After classes got over, we all assembled in the college ground. The students were hugging each other. I was at a distance from all this. Only one thing was going through my mind, only if I had not been a victim of the harsh realities of life, I too could have more friends like the others did. I wonder if anyone could have known how lonely I was feeling?

By now I had quit my job, so I would sit at home and recall those days at work. I was very passionate about calling up people and convincing them to buy our services. I recalled how on some days sales would materialize with ease, while on other days, despite taking approximately 400 calls I would not have the joy of a single buyer of our services. In addition to all this, there was so much always happening in the work milieu. Drama and tantrums were also a part of our work environment. I was treated like a rookie not till I closed a call and made sales on my own. This girl made me take her call and I did the price pitching feeling very nervous. The customer agreed and I was like, "yeah I did it!" After the call I went and hugged her, thanked her for trusting me and most importantly believing that I could do it.

People around us are not bad, rather it is the dominance of either the good or the bad in one that leads a person to becoming a good or a bad person.

Most importantly women are the force which can never be matched by a man. Everywhere – be it at home, work, school or any other institution they are more versatile when compared with men. We men are in fact dependent on them, but yet we strut our dominance over them.

My life is no different than most of you. It is very similar but I was eager to seek a way to touch an individual's life and make him or her move out from his/her shell and fight back. Accordingly, I have chosen to narrate and share the story of my life to encourage others in their times of hardship.

Trust me, we all are filled with positives and negatives, the most important challenge is to take measures to refine our strengths and become aware of, and work on, our negatives. Things can go right or wrong based on how we use our wisdom. Figure out your strengths and weaknesses and work on them accordingly. Having said this, don't ever forget that everyone is unique. Don't start considering only yourself unique and make others feel useless. We can only make things in our own lives and that of others' lives better if we cherish the uniqueness in each one of us.

For this to become a reality, you will have to take measures and align yourself to this thinking. Apart from the set of your own problems there are people who are facing problems of different kinds too. This presents us with a great opportunity and that is to voluntarily take charge of our own situation and persevere to make our problems an opportunity for us to grow and impart hope to those people who have given up.

We humans exist so that we can make things better for everyone around us. If we confine ourselves within our own narrow outlook, nothing can be gained in meaningful terms.

When I was working while at University, I realized that my taking charge of my University expenses motivated many of my classmates to do the same. They gave me the moniker of being a fighter.

Yet, as for me, I was extremely eager to be where they were and to be able to laugh in a carefree manner like they did. Did I not deserve to laugh like that? There was just too much of a burden on my shoulders. I continued going to the pond near my home when evening would fall. There I would cry my heart out.

If I am to describe my state of mind at that point in time, it was very melancholic. I was hopeless and desperately wanted the moon and stars to emerge in the darkness, to shine and lighten up my life, just like they shone bright in the night sky. With cigarettes in my pocket and music loaded on my mobile, all I would do is sit there and smoke, listen to the music, remain quiet for sometime till tear drops rolled down my cheeks.

I wanted a solution for my own problems only and for the rest of the world, I said, "Who cares?" This was the reason why my growth started getting hindered. You just cannot think of growth if you are self-centered and confined in your own world. You might find a solution to your problems but is it all that you want? To many youngsters who dream of growth but are mired in their problems, they need to stop looking for mediocre solutions and aim high. How do you do this?

First make the word problem synonymous with opportunity, and pounce on it just like a lion latches on to its prey. While you do all this, make sure you also do the act of assuring other people that even their problems will turn into opportunities. You see when you do it this way, you become a hero, and your growth becomes a resource that restores hope amongst people.

However, that's not it, it is an ongoing process that must continue for the rest of our lives. Only by forging ourselves with this spirit, we can exceed our own capabilities. Isn't that something we want?

When I was studying assiduously during my boards, my only goal was to get what I wanted but what after that? My grave mistake was not to continue in the same manner. As a result, I lost that spirit of persevering and thereby even lost out on an opportunity to achieve the impossible, thereafter.

It is easier to achieve your goals when persevering with a vibrant spirit but it is a challenge to sustain this perseverance throughout your life. People who are able to sustain this spirit become truly great. I read quotes by many people but they didn't really make sense to me. Quotes from great thinkers are not really a substitute to the learning we can get from real life experience.

Those who love quotes and follow them are in reality crippling themselves from not only the teachings that real life experiences offer but they also reduce their own chances of exploring life in a way that is unique to them.

Once college got over, I started wondering about my life ahead? See, I was again so clueless about my goals in life. I believe when you are still clueless about the purpose you want to live for, the best idea is to pursue whatever is at hand with all your heart. Amidst this pursuit only one can discover his/her purpose in life. This is what I did. I started watching movies on Mahatma Gandhi and Bhagat Singh.

Apart from the movies, I wanted to grow in my Buddhist practice as this was a joyful exertion. This practice required seeking faith through daily efforts in three areas namely faith, practice, and study.

Members here sought human revolution. In troubled times, the way for each one of them was to focus on their own human revolution. It is like changing yourself from within to make coping with things in the external environment easier.

I cannot forget the initial days when I would travel long distances to attend Buddhist meetings and that too with a minimal amount of money.

I wanted to change myself for my own good and this was the exact tool I needed. Embrace each human in your environment and develop compassion and courage, the usage of which is entirely based on one's own wisdom.

Our mentor, Daisaku Ikeda is an example of how any human being can accomplish phenomenal goals by basing every single aspect of it on faith. I could relate with him purely because like me he too underwent severe hardship during his teenage years. What he underwent was more severe. He lost his elder brother during the Second World War, his entire family was in distress and from there on he took up this faith with a determination to eradicate misery from this world. He succeeded through constant efforts in polishing his own life during his youthful days.

What I learnt from him was that even though you have dealt with severe problems in life and people have made you feel terrible, after overcoming your problems you not only become victorious but also develop an outlook that shows much gratitude to these people and your difficulties because of which you come to define a new and very unique perspective towards life. In a nutshell, developing compassion at such moments was what he emphasized on.

I can go on talking about the philosophy and my mentor but the important thing my readers must bear in mind is that the whole idea behind this book was my mentor whose writings encouraged me at a time when I was very low. You should appreciate and revere a person who stands by you during your worst times. Ikeda Sensei, my mentor was, and will, always be that person to me.

Why do we have mothers and why do they know so much about us? Mothers know us inside-out. My mother was no different. She told me several times that anyone can fool you and use you. I did not want to believe her when she said so.

I always wanted to be that cool guy who would be like the most sought after boy by a girl. However, all the girls I tried getting along with had one thing in common to talk about me and that was my child-like nature. This for them was a reason for being with me in relationships that were short-lived. Perhaps I was too honest about my feelings, about how I felt being with a girl I loved.

I tried everything possible to make my girlfriend happy. I wanted her to smile and be my companion, and together we could win the battle of hardships. But this never happened. In today's world there are girls who don't want just feelings and love. I could not understand this logic then and believed that if I make my woman happy it should be all that she could want. Maybe I was getting into the wrong relationships.

If I am to be honest, they used me for their own pleasure. The saddest part was when it was time to end it, they would simply walk away, with no words said at all.

I would share every bit of it with my mother and she would time and again tell me about my areas of vulnerability. She would also tell me that I was a special son and special people don't have small things in their lives. They are meant to achieve big goals and live their dreams. She told me one fact and that is the most important thing I always hold in my heart, love happens without a word being conveyed. This is why love is unique.

After I broke up with my last girlfriend on my birthday night I could not hold my tears back and kept asking myself why in the world did she not understand my love for her? Were all those kisses and hanging out together hand in hand nothing but fake? Sitting beside a pond which was so dear to me, I would question myself and lament upon each moment I spent with her.

When upset, she would go crazy and start biting my fingers for no reason and even then I would not stop her from doing it. She would often grab my waist from behind and say, "Yuvi I love you". I can never forget that evening when she was crying and I licked her tears saying, with a lot of passion, that they were all mine. Was doing all of this not enough for her to understand that I loved her? Maybe her expectations of me were way too high and I could not meet them.

My life, my buddy, Pranam would meet me often after my break up and he would come up with strong reasons why I should not feel bad, even in the remotest sense, about all that had happened.

He stood beside me like a pillar. When in a relationship, I would give all kinds of excuses to him because I wanted to be with the girl I loved and I ignored my own life and friends as a result.

Sitting on the benches in a tea shop we would smoke cigarettes and would talk of all possible things that I could do to overcome that phase.

One fine day, my father came to know about all this and told me that because I was truthful about my relationship to him, he was proud to be my father.

All of this made me ponder about myself and hence I was determined to never fall for another girl again. I decided that if I was to live for anyone then it was for nobody but for my family and my closest friend, Pranam.

It took me a couple of months to really get back to normalcy but when I did, I never thought about her. I realized that her going away from my life opened up a lot of avenues for me. These avenues were opportunities to explore my own purpose and my own goals in life. Instead of hatred, I started expressing my immense gratitude to her through my prayers.

When we are in love, the mere illusion that firstly governs our entire system is a notion of it being the entire thing we really want for the rest of our lives. After my breakup, I realized how tied down I had become in just trying to keep my relationship afloat. In lieu of trying to do this, I lost some happy moments with my parents and also missed out on something meaningful that could have been accomplished then. However, it was a lesson I learnt and made up my mind to never compromise on my dreams and most importantly my parents' happiness.

My friendship with Pranam was growing and we both loved being with each other. We both felt that we understood each other's feelings very well.

How pure is friendship? The purity level of friendship cannot be understood until we have one such friend in our lives. It is not just about partying or having food together but it is much more than that. Hearts beat for each other and one's pain is felt by the other person without even expressing it. You fight but it gets over soon because neither of you feel good about being away from each other.

Friends, be it love or friendship both these terms are divine and to take anyone of these casually will definitely ruin the future you are thinking of. However, at times, when you are supposed to take a stand and your love or friendship is at stake, you must be wise enough to vouch for something that is just. If this jeopardizes your relationship then trust me, the other person never understood you because one who cannot appreciate your reasons for taking such a stand can only be counted as a person in a relationship with you but with a tag of conditions applied.

All of this learning has come to me through experience and not by merely reading good quotes from successful people. Learning from every mistake is a source which helps us nurture our lives and live life with prudence. If mistakes happen let them happen but once you realize your mistake vow to never repeat it again. If you do repeat it then it's foolishness and trust me none of us like being called foolish. Since my school days in Nepal, I have always hated this word.

Although this experience of work was very short lived, I just cannot ignore talking about it. During graduation, I started working for a firm that was into manufacturing sockets. I used to fill up the statutory forms and also pay wages to the workers. Apart from this, I would travel to industries where I would be awed seeing the managerial people out there.

It was monsoon then so while returning home I would get drenched in the heavy rain. This would irritate me.

I would reach office and stretch my legs because I was exhausted. The humidity in Calcutta is really pathetic. It sucks out the fluid from your body and drains you in no time, and my boss would make things worse for me. The number of silly mistakes I committed made him yell at me every day.

Why was I making mistakes? Why was I travelling long distances to get a purchase order signed? Everything that I did was because of my feet. They always wanted to walk because somehow they knew that this was the only way I could forge myself into a strong and capable individual. This is why I say that to continue walking is so important. Refraining from walking would have let me be the way I was and never change things from misery into a source of joy.

When I left this job, the only thing I realized was the necessity to work for myself. We can easily put blame on others but they don't bring any change and change is much more important than blaming. Blaming others for your misery can only bring ignorance and make you more of a complainer.

How hopeless could I get? Why was it always happening with me? Why were my friends not dealing with something of this kind and why was I facing this seemingly relentless struggle? Then I did not have any answer to these questions but today when I look back I find that all those moments make a lot of sense to me and instead of questions I have gratitude for having being someone who faced it all.

What is the reason for which I was born? Why am I doing what I am doing? And what is the end goal of life? I sought answers to all these questions from my conscience. I was very much into myself. Always criticizing my actions and trying to do my best at whatever came my way was pivotal for me. When I would fail, I would go into a zone where I would curse myself and hit myself as much as I could.

I was doing all this to better myself. Even today, if anything goes wrong in my work I sit down and really start introspecting so that I can identify the areas where I went wrong. Even after that some people around me don't stop blaming me or ridiculing me for some time. This however stops when I take corrective measures and make amends.

It was not the case then. All I would do was brood and kick myself more than anything else. It took me a while before I realized that I had to take some action and check my own conduct and, if wrong, correct it.

This is how I have been able to make more friends and have people who listen to me. No matter how great you are at something until you don't take steps to correct your flaws, people will walk away from your life and no one will listen to what you have to say. This is harsh but it is true.

I would urge you to not just read this book and put it on your library shelf. Please don't do that. Instead experiment with some of the steps I have talked about and you will surely be able to understand how this works in a practical sense.

Money matters can make you feel worse. They still do in my case. I imagine a world where smiles could replace money and bonds of friendship and trust are more important.

After a hiatus again I had an encounter with money woes and this time it was worse than ever.

I did not score well in my CAT Entrance exams so I had to settle for a decent college from where I could get an MBA degree. I was shortlisted by a few of them. Hey, do you want to know the reason why I could not do well in the CAT exam? Well, the mere fact that I did not prioritize well was a prime reason why I scored poorly.

Even failing here did not stop me from moving ahead. I wanted to give up but like all times, this time too my feet did not want to stop, they wanted me to continue walking. So, I now started looking at banks which could give me an education loan.

To be honest, there are so many laws and provisions under which one can procure a loan for higher studies. However, I found it to be all on paper only. In future I hope people in desperate need of an education loan do not face what I went through.

Only providing loans to students whose parents have good bank records or providing it to only those who qualify for the IITs (Indian Institute of Technology) or IIMs (Indian Institute of Management) is the case. Where do the ones who were unlucky with scores and don't have enough money to afford higher education go?

My father did not have any bank account and it was only my mother who had a bank account but her bank statements were not sound enough to help me procure a bank loan.

How did things work out then? Well, all of us were trying our best. I went to as many banks as possible. Seeing their adverts I thought it was possible for me to get a loan easily but the adverts and the ground reality in banks were worlds apart. Although I did not succeed, my feet told my heart that you just cannot stop or give up like this. I yelled at myself but even then my feet were so firm in their belief that they never let me quit.

I always keep a close eye on my feet, somehow they have a divine power it seems. They never fail to communicate to my falling spirit that I am yet to cross the line.

Every time I would fall and feel the necessity of having someone who could pat me for a while and make me feel better, sadly it would never happen. My feet would even then tell me to stop brooding or craving for sympathy and fight this out because "you are not a loser. You are born to win."

Out of all the miseries, there was one misery that I always had nerve breaking moments about. I was always in search of that one person together with whom I could face all the challenges that surrounded me. A girl, whom I had become friends with, seemed to be a good person. Somehow, after a week or so, she stopped talking to me for no reason. In the ending days of my relationship, my girlfriend's behaviour made me suffer from a serious nervous breakdown. She would not tell me a thing about what she was up to and I would keep guessing all possible reasons. In this case my feet went numb in front of the might of a girl whose behaviour was only feeding doubts in my mind.

I later realized how fragile and dependent I was in spite of having proven that I was strong in many ways. This made me realize the inner work I still had to do on myself. We all must do the same, harping on our strengths and ignoring our weaknesses can only create problems.

This work of strengthening our weaknesses will continue for the rest of our lives and this is one reason why life is a journey and not a destination.

We need to understand that the world we live in today is harsh. However, we need to survive and ignorance will not help. The only fact that can help in erasing some bit of harshness or all of it is to not be ignorant. Most of the time, we ignore our parents' advice and after a while we say to ourselves, "If only I had…" stop doing that. Ignoring is next to escapism in my view. You might be able to ignore a problem and move on but the problem will not leave you.

So, we must not adopt escapist ways because it is nothing less than slow poison. Let us face it with boxing gloves in our hands and beat it harder every single time.

If you don't want to follow my words that is absolutely fine with me only if you are following your heart. Somehow, it knows very well about what is to be done with regards to the problems we face. Why don't we resort to it and take opinions from it rather than waiting for some senior professor or counselor to help us out. Your heart knows you more than anybody else. No counselor or psychiatrist can understand your pain, that too in a few hours. The story of your life is to be written by you so don't let yourself fail.

My feet – talking about it seems so flimsy but believe me, I have a strong friendship with them. They made me walk, walk through tough phases of my life and empowered me to see and forge a way, through challenges, for myself.

It is always important to learn from people around you. My parents and some of the people I met have helped me in learning various things like becoming disciplined. Today, everything that I do is purely based on time. How can I make the entire 24 hours in a day count? This is a prime question I keep answering every single day the result of which will be visible after a period of years. This solely means that it needs constant effort.

Efforts made by us are important. My feet always told me about the importance of effort and how with utmost, sincere effort one could achieve the impossible. This was my sole intent. The efforts of my father in whose eyes I saw utmost concern for getting me admitted in a B-School, made me realise how wrong I had been to have always ridiculed my father and to never have appreciated his efforts. He loved me more than anybody else in the world. For him it was through me that he wanted to see his dreams come true. He did not show emotions of love and care much but that moment when I saw him discuss the funding of my education with a relative, I watched his eyes and was most touched by his concern for me.

Friends, whatever mistakes you commit never make the grave mistake of hurting your mother and father. These two people are the most pure hearted souls we have been gifted with in our lives. Respect them when you are young and love them when they grow old. That is all they want from you.

My friendship with Pranam will always be special. When someone walks up to you and offers you his/her hand in friendship I sincerely believe that such people should always be cherished with an open heart. We laughed, cried, fought and did many such things together. We smoked in almost every street of Calcutta. Name a street and we have certainly smoked there.

We spent a lot of time talking, even if the conversation was on inconsequential topics. Even though the conversation was casual it bought us closer together as friends. There were times when we would also talk about how we could make things better to progress in our lives. The most important topic was how do I make my girlfriend realize that I love her? At such times, one of us would be scratching his head because in reality nothing came into our heads and we would simply remain confused.

We both were love seekers but our girlfriends were in need of something more than just love. Emotions overpowered us on various occasions but even then together we tried to problem solve. Hence, it wouldn't be wrong to say the women in our lives brought us closer together as friends. We met very often and this was why our parents were not happy with the kind of connection we started developing. However, we both were family loving people so we often talked about family happiness and what it meant to us.

After meeting his family and getting to know them, I realized that even if you are rich what matters is humility. They always treated me like their own son and made sure that I was present on special occasions. Just like my mother and father they would scold me for any wrong doing. We both smoked a lot and that was worrying our parents a great deal.

While sitting down to chat at a shop near his home, we smoked cigarettes in bulk. A packet would take no time to finish. I know this was an unhealthy habit. However, we loved each other a lot. We could sense each other's upset without words. Our hearts spoke to each other most of the time. If I am to be honest, great moments can never be described in words. They can only be lived. I am not good enough in phrasing words but I surely know and can speak about it with joy – that we both rocked together.

Even though we parted ways for our respective MBA courses, we were both very united at heart even then. My father's words made a deep impact on my mind. He said, "Do everything but now the whole of our family is counting on you. "So, make us proud."

I was there with him when he convinced some relatives of ours to lend us some money so that I could start with my course. He was willing to do anything to get me there. It seemed as if it was his very own dream to see me become a MBA graduate.

He never learnt to stop when it came to getting a job at hand done. Maybe his feet never allowed him to give up. Certainly, it is from him that my feet have inherited this trait. Even though I am talking here about inheritance but the key truly lies in believing that things will happen. Even if everything is dark and gloomy right now, I know I will see the light. I will win. I might have lost my path but that is when I will rediscover myself. So, I have to keep moving and never stop. Stopping is death and I don't want to die so soon.

This is what my feet told me while I was left alone in the crowd to deal with not just big problems but with colossal miseries. Does a 15 year old ever imagine being told that his time for education is over and now it is time to work and earn? When a shop owner scolds you for not understanding what he said, how do you think a 15 year old would feel?

Believe me then I cried, I cried my heart out, sitting beside a pond in the dark. Nobody saw me, nobody heard me but I felt good after that because my feet not only persisted on rising up again and continuing to walk but also gave me the pat on my back I craved from some of my nearest and dearest.

When I go on writing about all that I have to share with all my readers, I will constantly keep answering one question in various ways. Why am I writing this book? Not to make money, not to see publicity coming my way or my photo in a well known magazine or a newspaper. The idea behind it was simple and straight.

You see, there are crucial moments when we seek hope and encouragement from someone. I want to be that someone for you. People keep asking me what my life purpose is and after all the trauma and fire fighting episodes I see this as my sole purpose in life and this is what I am living for. Not just because I know of ways to deal with it but mostly because I have all throughout my times of struggle learnt to be more humble and more compassionate.

We both friends were now away from each other but our intent to succeed was very palpable. I made up my mind to never think of the past and consider myself now as a new born baby wanting to exceed limits and discover himself.

Gurgaon was a new place to me but I got used to it very soon. I did not go out much because I knew that I had to carry on my expenses for a month with the money I got from home. It was not a big deal for me to cut down my expenses and be a conservative boy.

Once you understand the value of Re.1, you are sure to realize how tough it is to make an honest earning. I know it very well because for me there were times when even a penny or say even a grain of rice mattered a lot.

Mentally I was sure of what I had to do. Work hard, learn a lot of things and make this phase a gateway to become a learned man who wanted to learn more, no matter where the learning came from. I was harsh to myself. There were presentations and discussions on various topics governing the business world. I made sure that I was prepared for any topic.

Why did I do all this? You see at graduation level money was my aim, while the aim of my classmates was to grasp knowledge and ideas which would help them for the rest of their lives. I took being away from home as an opportunity to strengthen my knowledge repertoire and to do my best. However, I did not have friends. I say so because a friend does not just respect you. They also laugh with you and hang out with you. With me here, it was different. I was alone but my inner self always yearned for knowledge. I would sit with professors and discuss various topics. If I did not understand something, I would get to know it from scratch just like a child. I wanted to be the best.

There was a test that our economics professor took and I was well aware of the answers of it. Many of them in the class did not know the answers. I helped some of them around me with the questions.

When the results came, I failed with the lowest marks in the class. I was called by the professor to his cabin. He handed me my mark sheet and told me to learn English. I had my eyes wide open when he said so. He was very rude too. I came out of his cabin and did not attend any other lecture that day. I bought myself a packet of cigarettes and went into my room. I jumped into bed and smoked a cigarette.

I have always been a critic of my own deeds. Every time I am made to feel bad by anyone I retreat and become self critical. I criticize myself for some time and very soon I start taking measures to make sure that I not only don't repeat it next time but I exceed the expectations of people and affirm their belief that I have worked on myself.

We should never be ignorant towards people who give us valuable feedback. If you see it this way, in today's world when all are so busy and preoccupied with their own duties and work, why would someone take the initiative and make the time to give your their feedback? Such feedback, when received, serves as a tool that can aid us to change for the better. I know my act of coming back and smoking was not a good one. However, after a while I became determined to work from scratch and I made sure I work on excelling at economics.

I started reading articles from great economic gurus, economics related magazines and tried to understand every bit of it just like a small child. I deepened my study of economics and vowed to become proficient in the subject very soon.

You see, the kind of situation my professor put me into I could have ignored him saying, "This old man is crazy". However, I did not do that. Rather, I took his criticism as the impetus to improve my grasp over economics. Sometimes, we presume ourselves to be too good at something, such that we forget the need to keep ourselves grounded and, most importantly, to always remain a learner.

Applying my inner wisdom to work really hard on economics helped me to not only score better marks but it drew the attention of my beloved professor. He recognized the kind of effort I put to improve myself. Even my class mates starting coming to me for help in matters related to the subject.

I had my own ways of explaining. I always insisted on self work and self effort. The conjoint effort put in this way cannot only help you master the subject but bring the subject alive. The mastered principles can then become transferable to the real world. The fear within us sometimes inhibits us and can even overshadow our self belief. Experiencing fear is natural but it is important to not let it stop us from forging ahead. The time of youth is a time of struggle, of perseverance and if we fail to overcome our fears at this stage in our lives, the years to come will bear this out.

Ask anyone around you who is in his/her 40's and seems to possess a magnet like personality, about his youth and s/he will tell you of the hardwork s/he put in, work that enabled better years ahead for him/her. So now the question to be answered is how does one get rid of the fear within oneself and start believing in oneself? In this case, my answer is a well thought out one. Ask your heart to help you. Yes ask it for it knows how you actually can beat fear and start believing. Don't resort to quotes and pictures on google which contain quotes of great thinkers. I say so purely because even the great thinkers followed their hearts.

At times, we fail to realize how assertiveness can become a reason for our failures. It is important that we pay attention to people who speak to us purely out of genuine concern. Being ignorant towards such people will only pave the way for disharmony and discord. At times, when someone does anything that is unethical, it is important that we speak up. If we remain ignorant, we become perpetrators together with the culprits. Ignoring the genuine concern of people and ignoring the wrong doings of people around us might seem to be insignificant but they have an enormous impact on the larger framework of society today. People who say ignorance is bliss are the ones who have found ways to escape the realities of life and the weaknesses present in them.

If I gave it back to my professor, bitterness amongst both of us would have grown. Not being ignorant to his opinion allowed me to work religiously to better my grasp of economics. Very soon he was able to realize my level of hard work to improve my command over my favourite subject. Very soon, we became friends and would discuss economic and political issues very often even after classes got over.

Even you my friend can do it and perhaps in a bigger way. It is only your heart that can help you do so. The only thing one needs to do is replace ignorance with genuine concern.

If you want to know of ways which can help you turn poison into medicine, the only thing that can be of help is your courage and your sincere efforts. Many a times, we think that our sincere efforts yield us no benefit so it is necessary to resort to unfair tactics. To some extent, that is true. To a greater extent it is false, very false. The world operates on the phenomenon of cause and effect, so if I am giving something my all out sincere effort, how foolish would I be to even think that the results will not be meaningful?

It is like when I give my all to a given task and the result of it may or may not be favourable. In both the cases, I win because even if I have lost on the results front, the lessons I have learnt by giving it my best shot brings a great deal of satisfaction to me.

Now viewing it the other way round, if I don't give a task my best effort then even expecting things to apparently work in my favor is stupidity. This is like seeking sympathy to somehow get over the line. Even though I hate it, my hatred towards such stupidity won't change things a great deal. It actually is all on us, whether we want to be courageous like lions or remain a coward.

Sitting on the roof top in the middle of the night, I would constantly ask myself, how do I change my parents' situation from one filled with hardships into one filled with hope and joy?

One night while on our way home at night, I saw my father holding a bag containing samples of products, heavier than one would imagine. It surely was not less than 15 or 20 kgs. Walking behind him, I could see him wiping his sweat with one hand and holding the bag in the other. Very spontaneously, I was grinding my teeth and telling myself, "I am ashamed to see you do all this even when you have a son who is fully fit to start earning and do every bit for your happiness. Dad, those days are not far when you will not need to labour so hard but instead will have the luxury of rest with my mother in a grand bungalow. I will do my best to make this vision a reality."

My parents are sources of strength who always encourage me to push myself irrespective of whether things are easy or tough.

Every night in Gurgaon before going to sleep, I would say to myself, "Mom I am doing this for you. Please always smile and be as loving as you have always been."

Sadly, many of us don't even have our parents with us in which case we need to do for ourselves what our parents would have done for us, that is, we need to fortify ourselves with strength. Problems test one of our two sides: which are firstly, giving up and secondly, enduring even when you are surrounded by darkness.

When you enter a dark tunnel you continue to walk until you see light. So by pushing yourself an inch further while you are wanting to give up can stop you from losing the battle. Believing in the fact that death is inevitable and thereby living each moment to its fullest can assure us of not only overcoming our trivial problems but it also leads us to proudly proclaim on our deathbed, "I lived my life to the fullest".

I know many amongst us have become so hopeless that we don't even wish to live. I don't pity you at all. I only want to meet you to give you all logical reasons why you should fight back. I can spend the rest of my life encouraging people to fight back. There are people who are so into their own lives in a self centered way that they forget the most meaningful benefit they would derive is helping their friends who are depressed or feeling isolated. One thing that all of you reading this book should remember is that when you raise someone else's hand, your hand goes up too.

Which means empower anyone around you and what you will see is your own life shining with the spirit of courage and compassion and, in the process, your perspective towards life will deepen.

We have somehow forgotten what our teachers at school and parents at home taught us, that is, to help others and treat others with a sense of equality. To be precise, we urgently need to introspect within ourselves and wonder if we are doing our part in believing in every individual's potential. If not, we are not only demeaning them but are primarily demeaning ourself. Think of it logically and you will understand what I mean.

The result of an action will respond to the approach we adopt towards it. Most of us understand this fact but we still continue to lament, complain about our circumstances and act passively.

I say this because even I have had times when I wanted to be passive towards an issue at hand. After a while, I would sense that the result attained is exactly according to the effort put in by me. Yes, there were times when despite my sincere effort, I would not attain the desired result. This is what helped me understand that an active approach does not always help you become a winner but at times, it teaches you something that is more than just winning. You might not have won but in essence you are still a winner.

During classes, I would try and be more focused and with a sincere heart devote myself to understanding what the teacher was teaching and absorb it well. I would do this to such an extent that I would get into the smallest aspect of a topic to begin my understanding from there.

I realized that I was a slow learner and required a lot of individual effort to understand a topic. Teachers would be delighted when I did not raise my hand to ask a question. Even if friends around me felt it caused them much irritation I still continued doing what I was doing. You see if you want to know something you should not keep quiet and wait for the teacher to approach you to ask if you have any problems. The first step taken is a sign of courage and one who hesitates just because people around him/her might bully them are not doing any good. Let us come out of our shells and do what we are meant to do. If others know it very well but I don't know it then there is absolutely no need to worry. Just approach your mentor and seek his/her help, if he refuses see if your friend can but if nobody is willing to help you then well, you are in the process of discovering your own potential as a self tutor.

No one from home was with me but their expectations were always felt. If I as their child expected them to make my wishes come true then even they at some point have the right to expect me to deliver and bring happiness to them, especially during their old age. Whenever I felt like giving up, I would think of my mother who was herself a fighter. Even today she does not dwell on people's views that are sans hope. She is an inherently hopeful and optimistic person and her actions reflect this. Start respecting women for their inner strength. Don't command them, instead support them just like they support you. My mother and my father were people who encouraged me and always made me strive for the best results during my MBA.

At times when I would be lazy or the weather would be very cold, I would also try to escape from assignments and look for lame excuses. However, when I did so, I would scold myself repeatedly. Determined to never repeat such acts I would start doing things all over again. So, I kept getting back to the basics and making some much needed changes to get exceptional remarks or comments for any project or case study that I undertook. This was all possible because though I was far I was living every single moment for my family.

In life you have to live for some goal or for somebody. If you don't then you will see that even though you achieve your goals, after a while you will be clueless about what is the next thing you should aspire for. This was a lesson I learnt from my mistake during the first year of graduation. After that I did not make this mistake again because I started living my life for a purpose and that was for my mother and my father.

It is not necessary that you too have the same purpose as I have. What is important, is to at least have one purpose in life for which you are willing to give your very best.

I was alone there, I hardly had any friends. What I had was a purpose for which I was only putting my best step forward. Even if setbacks arose, they did not trouble me for long. This is the benefit of living for the fulfillment of your life purpose. When you live with this mindset, no trivial matters can faze you for long.

When you and I know that our lives are filled with moments of joy and sorrow then in no way should we feel bad about any problem at hand. Instead, we should use it as a means through which we can grow. In short, every problem is actually an opportunity to grow.

However, many of us are hesitant to even accept such opportunities. We avoid them at all times, making us more vulnerable and prone to being fearful all the time. Even I tried doing the same when I had come to Calcutta. It did not work out well. At last, I realized the only recourse was to accept this challenge, to go through the rough patches but to focus on the bigger picture.

When we play a video game, we work to clear level after level to win in the end. Similarly, when it comes to dealing with problems the same concept applies. You win over a problem and you find that there are other problems ahead. So problems, in a sense, are relentless. The more you challenge your problems, the more you will grow. If you don't do this, you become a quitter and not a fighter. It is that simple.

I am no saint or sage. I am just one of you. I too feel hopeless and in need of some support at times. However, now I rely less on outside support. But I did not reach this stage of self reliance overnight. It took a lot out of me to get here. I have been hit really hard and to pick myself up was always difficult but I realized that once I picked myself up there was no way I would look back. Diligent effort is what you need. Many of us are doing this without our conscious realization.

What is more joyful – a road that leads you straight to the top or a road that has rough roads, rocks and hurdles of all kinds? You very well know what I mean when I say this. Many of us, nevertheless, seek easy ways out in life. There is no harm in seeking an easy route but the inner strength and the aspect of forging oneself is more evident in the case of routes that are tough and full of hardships. Your parents are living examples in this regard. Sit and try to understand if they could do it, then why is it not possible for you to do it?

Bear one important thing in mind, nobody is born confident and knows all from day one of his/her birth. So you don't need to hesitate about continuing your walk. Only after staying with 'your walk' for a period of time, you will realize how much you have grown. The level of confidence that you presume to be absent in you today will be at its prime level. A level where nobody can bring you down because by then you have done the most important thing in life – that is to conquer yourself.

Don't seek sympathy or help from people around, even if they offer it to you, reject it at once. I say so because all of this only makes you dependent on them by diminishing the possibility of empowering yourself.

Hopelessness was prevalent all around me. Come on, if you see a boy who is not even capable of paying his school fees, you won't in all honesty be sure of whether he will be able to even complete his formal education. All of us possess a deluded mind, even I did. However, I did not stop to smile on certain occasions nor did I say that I am not trying it only because I did not have the resources.When the degree of hopelessness would increase, my efforts to keep walking would also increase. If I ever got exhausted, I spoke to myself sitting beside a pond and I made myself feel a bit lighter so that I could continue with renewed strength. This was how I kept continuing my walk which will continue till my last breath.

Your walk might lead you to your destination but our journey of life is never a destination, is it? So continuing to walk is a journey. Your walk can only become a journey if you are striving along with people who too are striving in some way or the other. Self centered focus for growth is shallow and leads one to a form of success which is transient. When you are empowering someone to strive and you yourself have belief and courage, your growth as a human being becomes exponential. Honestly speaking, if this starts happening then no one will be in need of a motivational speaker and no one will ever have to write a motivational book.

Ever since I came to Calcutta, life threw myriad challenges to pulverize me. I would sleep in a playground because at home things were hard for me to bear. At school, I did not speak to a single student. Teachers thought that I was dumb but how would I go and tell them that all I was experiencing seemed surreal even to me. Every time I would go to approach a well learned and a rich person for help so that I could study, I would feel a tremendous sense of pain within me. I would come back and unburden my feelings on my mother and my father. When I was in college, I wanted to learn new things but the financial situation at home was not sound so I took up a job in a call center. Why did I do all this?

I have an answer to this. When situations get really bad, your true character and capability get tested. We feel so helpless that we don't want to get up and seek sympathy from people around us. Believe me it does no good but only makes you dependent. I am thankful that I had no one around to sympathize with me. Maybe that's why a possibly uncertain situation attracts me more today. A challenge coupled with some fear makes me see an opportunity in it. When I walk down 10 kms at a stretch, I feel happy to see people all around me.

You decide what is it that you want to do. Sit back and hold on to your grief, sorrows or the breakup that you have recently had or make this given situation a reason for you to rise up as a much stronger person? Let this world know what you are made of. Even when you succeed in your attempt, don't develop a shallow heart by treating people wrongly. Instead show gratitude to them and see if you can make them feel hopeful. This way you will surely multiply your prospects of becoming an individual who infects people with positivity. Compassion, courage and wisdom are three vital ingredients that transform the worst situation into a situation where not only are we empowered but others around us are also empowered. So don't you think this way you can create a harmonious society and make this world a better place?

Now for all this, you need to make all your worries, anguish and anxiety a resource to push yourself and seek the opportunities that lie ahead. I will keep telling you this all the time. "Every problem that comes our way presents us with an opportunity to grow. However it depends on us if we take that opportunity or not."

There are many people who have negative beliefs about themselves – that they are unlucky or things just never work out for them. When I was 15, even I had such negative views towards life. This belief pattern continued till I was 23. After each year its level started diminishing. It had to be that way because I was not willing to take things just because of the way they were.

From being a sweeper to an MBA graduate, when I look back every incident that happened then seemed to have its own meaning. But at the time, I would feel as if the world had crashed upon me because nothing of that sort happened to other people I knew.

However, today it is different. I don't get perturbed by difficulties any more. Moreover, I try to be compassionate towards people who are facing tough situations. Succinctly put, this is helping me in my personal growth and development.

We have started seeing growth as being synonymous with economic growth. However, as you see yourself step into the real world, you will surely realize that monetary growth fades after a while. I believe most of us have heard this saying, "When you die, people remember you not for the money or the parties you threw but surely for the kind of person you were".

I did not know the tricks but I knew how to give my best and the theory to be able to do so is simple – sheer diligence and devotion. You might find people who use their smartness to bring quick positive results. Should that not affect me? No, it should not. I say so not because I disrespect such people, rather I say so because I don't compare myself with others. Their victory is theirs.

All of us are unique and are born with different talents. We might not be great with academics but we might be the best at sports or music or something else. So, let us initiate this walk of life every single day with a desire to only do our best even if we are not sure of when the light of hope will illuminate the darkness. It is without any doubt that I can strongly assert that we will find the real purpose of life this way. And everything that has brought you so much pain now will transform and joy will come your way.

Even if your walk is not confident enough now don't stop walking, for if you continue you will give your life the direction it truly deserves. If you stop, however, you won't be anything lesser than a person who has died while living.

During the first semester of my MBA course, I had a group of friends with whom I studied the whole night. Any chapter that seemed to be hard for anyone would be explained by the one who knew that chapter thoroughly. Most of you must have done it too during your college days. What was important was the lesson I learnt then. I understood that it is always easy to walk and grow alone but it is difficult to grow along with each other. However, if compassionate efforts are made then collective growth becomes possible.

Why can't we smile? Why can't we break the shackles of despair? Why do we talk about problems and more problems and not focus on the solutions? Why can't we just be a little more courageous so we can live for what we believe in? This world is going to be peaceful not if terrorism is stopped but only if we free ourselves from the narrowness and feelings of hopelessness that often become deeply rooted in our lives. Even the poem by Rabindra Nath Tagore titled, "Where the mind is without fear" talks of us being in charge of our own lives.

We tend to cry for what we don't have. Even I did this during my college days. I joined a call center because I did not have what my friends in college had. To be very candid, my purpose of living was shallow. However, my unrelenting spirit helped me in changing my mindset. Many of you won't agree but realizing your own mistakes is in itself a moment of courage and victory. This one life is what we know we have. So, if we keep complaining instead of doing something purposeful we will continue living mundane lives. Now living life to the full does not mean you become extravagant or flamboyant. When I talk of living life, all I mean is to live life with passion, enthusiasm and lots of courage and generosity and to do things with a sincere intent that create value in our society.

Even if you have suffered a lot you still can do a world of good by being empathetic towards others and by treating people, especially those who are suffering, with compassion and care. Such care is on the wane in our world today and to restore it we need to extend compassion towards all those around us. For your actions to create value you do not have to be a celebrity or a politician. As long as you have a vibrant spirit and a caring heart your individual good deeds, together with those of others, can turn around the destiny of mankind which today is replete with myriad anxieties.

So, let us jump out of our beds, wipe our tears, pick ourselves up and say I am not going to be defeated. Yesterday might have been a bad day and I can't do anything about it but by determining to live out my life to the fullest I am going to give my all out effort in making today productive.

You will sense an upsurge in your spirit which seemed to be dull and laid back. Do this every single day in the morning and you will notice a difference in how as a better and courageous human, your self-development becomes meaningful. Your uniqueness will surely manifest and you will keep growing and you will become a better person. What our society truly needs is good hearted people and this is how we can do it.

You might wonder how come I am saying this so convincingly. Yes I say this as I am fully convinced about how we can not only continue this walk of life, but also make this world a better place. At times, even my confidence is shaken. It is not that I don't suffer and I don't feel low. I do and I feel very despondent at times. In spite of this, I talk a lot to myself. I tell myself that I can't be like this. My life has a purpose and I am going to realize it no matter what happens. Then, after such self-talk I return to my winning ways. Doing this is actually easier than making your friends or people you know well believe in whatever you feel and mean. However, one should start from building one's self. It is only by doing this, that we can step ahead and not only empower others but also empower ourselves. How many times have you been happy after helping someone? The joy it brings to us is immeasurable.

If we are to meet the purpose of our lives then we must be courageous enough to fight back and stand tall. Even if we are left alone we still must be ready to face life head on. Most importantly, we must continue the walk inexorably.

No one believed me. Everyone once thought I was only a piece of waste. My relatives ignored me. My parents too doubted my potential many times. However, I stood firm and believed in my walk, in my journey. The one area where a constant level of effort was needed was in believing in myself and my determination to continue walking helped me do that.

My writings might not point you to a single conclusion, however, I hope you grasp the message I am conveying which is to persevere with a capital P. Today you might not be a brilliant student or a good communicator but you will succeed if you believe in yourself and in your ability to succeed and you persevere with this belief.

If you are someone who is an introvert don't feel bad about this. None of us are perfect. Secondly, even being an introvert means that you are a person who takes time to observe and understand things and then comment or act. To be precise, you are someone who talks less but whatever you say is meaningful. Also, if you are cautious about things you do that can be a positive thing too. You get into the minor details and make sure that everything feels right before going ahead on any project or assignment. In summary, we are all different personalities and that is why we are unique because you believe it or not but every single trait that you think of as negative in you, in reality, has its positive side too.

I always dislike my habit of being quiet all the time. My quietness became so extreme that I began feeling that people around me thought of me as a dumb person. However, after sometime, I realized how being quiet helped me internalize a particular thing profoundly and once that happened that very thing understood, became firmly lodged in my memory.

My MBA days taught me many lessons. In short, I underwent a transformation and for this, I feel a debt of gratitude towards my mentor Dr. Daisaku Ikeda, whom I have never met yet I keep striving to imbibe his spirit of being grounded and working with a strong belief in togetherness and courage. Like he says, "It is always the heart that matters the most". I too started applying his words in my daily life.

It was never an easy affair for me. Every single day I tried giving my best but instead of succeeding, I failed. I failed miserably. Why was it so? I felt like stabbing myself to death at times. There came a moment when I literally felt my rationale of sincere effort resulting in concrete results was shaken. However, the walk to succeed was never over. I continued, knowing that even if today was not my day tomorrow will be my day and I continued doing my best.

Comparisons were not something I appreciated. I wanted to exceed my own abilities. Being a slow learner and having a wandering mind were my biggest flaws that I wanted to work on. For this I did not use any specific tactic or strategy. What I used was the metaphor of continuing my walk. Yes, ways to work on it are important but if such ways don't work out then what matters is the willingness to persevere and make it happen.

There were moments when teachers became furious with me. On certain occasions I came across as an intelligent student and on some other occasions I was a dumb fellow. Whatever the situation, what mattered was the effort I was willing to put in not focusing on the end result at all. I felt if I work with utmost sincerity and passion it is assured that the result of it will be the best too but all of this will take its own time. So, the entire focus was to continue, to persevere at all costs. Even if death comes, our lives will still continue but in some other form. So, if a lesson of this kind is what I entirely base my life on, why would I ever stop continuing this walk?

All of this is so simple but simple things are never easy. You can continue with bad habits for a long time but to continue with one good habit is tough. It really is. I wish all of you were as philosophical as I am and speak to your feet more often to see where they can really take you.

Never does a bird that can fly say I don't want to fly. Similarly, your feet will never say that they wish to stop walking altogether. The day when we were born, our parents by default had their minds made up that come what may, we are going to give our lives to make our child the best we can. If they can have such resolve, why can't you have that too especially when you don't have as many responsibilities as your parents?

Things are right in front of us to internalize and implement. The only difference is our own realization. This has to come and it will come if we have our eyes set on a goal for which we are willing to make sacrifices. When we set such goals, our mission becomes clear and we constantly put efforts towards being able to accomplish them. These efforts result in the arrival of a day when, sitting on our death bed we can proudly say, "I lived my life". Many of us go by the facts or reality of life. If you ponder upon whatever I said above, all of it will seem to be both factual and realistic.

I knew that this MBA period can be made a turning point in my life through my efforts. I was eager to give it my all at all times. Nothing upset me or made me depressed for long because the goal set was a subset of a bigger goal in my life. I would look at my palm and say, "My past was terrible but my future is all on me to determine". There were various other ways like this which always provoked me to push myself a bit more every time.

How often does it happen that a happy situation at home or with friends turns into a disastrous one only because you have failed to impress them by living up to their expectations? It is not uncommon to feel bad and also become hopeless about our future under such circumstances but for how long should we feel despondent?

Long ago when we were children, our parents told us that every day is a new day. So when you wake up please smile and wake up, your day will go well. So, aren't we doing that? You see bad feelings arise because we are prone to getting affected by our circumstances. The worst thing we do in such a scenario is to put the blame on someone else instead of checking our own conduct and actions. Sadly, all of us do so but if it happens the other way round we can pave the way for our growth and continue our walk with a rejuvenated spirit.

You see, all of it is actually very simple. Those who say it is tough are correct in their context because they never want to believe otherwise.

I scored well in my first semester and right after it got over, I was packing my bags to go home. Seeing my family after six months made me feel so good.

When you are away from home, you feel nobody cares for you but when at home, one is showered with love. The reason for it is simple – your family love you and have missed you very much. Sometimes, I really wonder if we as children are doing enough for our parents. We say they are old fashioned and set them and their views aside. Yes, they are old fashioned but respect and, most importantly, appreciate the love they shower on you.

For them you are the world and love to them begins with you and ends with you. How are we reciprocating their love towards us?

The day I left for Gurgaon to resume my studies for the second semester I had a heavy heart. Somehow I could see my mother glowing like never before. When we did not have food or shelter to afford, I had seen her fight like a champion. I call her a powerhouse. Maybe I have taken after her and that's why I am strong.

When we want to be inspired, the best thing is to look at people around us. At times, even a handicapped person gives me courage and hope to continue this walk. I have feet to continue but he does not. Despite that if he can continue why can't I do the same?

Coming back and resuming my studies during the winter months was really tough. Everyone in my class would want to leave early because by 4 pm it was dark. I thought differently. I wanted to learn different aspects associated to economics and management. It was then that I thought of learning more. This learning was not confined to one subject but to different aspects of management or life.

Doing this, I slowly started realizing that life in itself was a lesson and if I wish to learn something, all I need is to become a good observer and a seeker of knowledge. At times, some of these people were instrumental in helping me pick myself up and continue my walk. How wonderful life can be? In fact it is very wonderful.

Having said that our trivial issues and problems appear in front us as a major constraint in advancing forward.

If we look within ourselves we will be able to realize how much these trivial issues and problems actually support us in widening our perspectives towards life.

However, while we seek new opportunities it is vital for us to not forget our other responsibilities. My desire to learn overtook my other responsibilities. The results thus obtained taught me a lesson very soon when my mid and second semester scores were very low.

In fact by the time the second semester results were out I was not in Gurgaon, I was in Chennai doing my internship which was to be an eventful experience that involved lots of learning. There were also awesome times with my best buddy, Pranam. However, my internship turned out to be very ugly.

No one was to be blamed for it but somehow as friends we started having differences in our views. In spite of hard times, we made it a point of not giving up on each other, believing that our bond is eternal and small hiccups like this are temporary. Even his sister was very supportive. While staying with her I realized a lot of things about girls. I was now able to see girls not as mere objects but as people who bring joy to every aspect of your life.

Getting into the details and understanding the depth of any matter is a habit I have since my school days. So, I would sit back and contemplate on the importance of women and the fact that despite this they are disregarded. Even then they don't complain. All of this realization was possible because of Samiksha Di. At times, she was livid with us but on occasions she would bestow all her love and affection on us. She was wonderful. My stay in Chennai was the best thing that happened to me, not for the happy moments we had but for all the weaknesses and vulnerabilities I realized were inherent in me. I had to do something about it. When

I returned from Chennai to Gurgaon after my internship got over I started introspecting on my actions and started working on every negative tendency I possessed. It took a while but eventually I was able to overcome this so called darkness that I feel I inherited.

One good thing that happened was now I was ready to face any challenge head on. Some of my friends in college noticed the kind of maturity I had developed. It was during this period that I felt like trying to be good to everyone around me. I am an introvert but during this phase I started opening up. I tried interacting with more people.

See friends, our lives have a purpose. To be very honest, people around us don't really understand our pain. It is only when one goes through it, is he or she able to empathize with us.

Reality is harsh. You might think that you can't do it or can't go ahead with life anymore. However, ask your feet whether you can or you can't? It will tell you not to stop. It only wants you to endure and persevere every single day. Hopes for a peaceful world rest on the youth. If youngsters are not hopeful about themselves to begin with then how will they fulfill their role in society/their country/in the world? I am talking of your spirit – that counts the most. The rest will follow, provided your intent is not to harm anyone. In my life, I encountered several incidents in succession.

If your entire focus is on growth then be ready to face obstacles and difficulties. While you endure them, don't ever forget that because you are growing you are facing difficulties. Endure it with a lot of heart and sincere effort. Victory will follow. However, do bear in mind that growing in life is a constant endeavor.

I wanted to grow exponentially and that is why perhaps I had to endure really harsh issues alone. I lost my laptop which was important to me. Within the span of a month I got viral fever twice and I had to stay at an uncle's place in New Delhi. Added to this, when I went home for Diwali, I was diagnosed with dengue and had to be in hospital for five days. It was in hospital that I realized the extent of my inner strength. The doctor on the very first day said that I have to be in the hospital for more than two weeks. I could sense the grief on the faces of my mother and father. They were upset but ready to accept reality. How could I let them be in grief when I was there? I optimistically told them that I would be out of hospital in five days. Deep within, I wanted to fight my own health issues to show to many people that if you desire something which can bring happiness to many people, it is always possible. To be precise, strength comes to those who live for others' happiness.

When I was discharged within five days, my parents were very happy and relieved. I could not have asked for more then. Even then both of them made sure that I was fully fit. I survived an accident I had before going back home. In a way, this event turned my entire perspective of life around.

The episode of the early morning accident tested my pain threshold – as I smiled despite the pain making people around me believe that nothing was wrong and I was alright. To be able to do that is also a sign of courage. Those stitches did not allow me to sit and study for my exams. Amit and Mrinal, towards whom I have immense gratitude kept encouraging me to have faith and challenge the situation. In a way, I had to win over my circumstances.

In many ways, they did the work of my feet, telling me to continue persevering. All my life, I have only learnt to do this.

Maybe this is why I don't expect anything from anyone. I feel the need to give hope and encouragement to people I encounter. This comes very naturally to me.

All that I endured, now are beautiful memories which have helped shape me as a person who feels the pain of the other person and treats it as if it were his own.

Giving up would not have made things better for me. Only enduring the walk and continuing to do so even now helps me shape myself into a man filled with hope and courage.

Many of us don't go through the same kind of problems but none of us can ever say with full confidence that we don't have problems. We all ought to have problems for it throws an open opportunity to strengthen our inner self more than ever, helping us to become compassionate and great individuals. Remember, I don't consider people who have dealt with harsh circumstances in their life and made their way to the top but fail to be compassionate towards others, as truly great. The narrow approach in their thoughts and actions are less valuable to me. People who have suffered the most and overcome their suffering while developing compassion for others who are suffering, are truly noble and great.

Life is large. If we allow petty episodes to rule our lives then certainly we are not living our lives to its fullest potential. All this learning that I am sharing with you has come about as a result of the events I've encountered in life. Even now I am learning more about life because learning from people around me is a perpetual process.

I don't find any difference between my walk down the road today and my walk then. To me it is like I have not even grown up but the in-depth understanding of problems people succumb to, is something which disturbs me to the core. Do me a favor, once you read this book and feel like keeping it on your book shelf, please don't do that. Hand this book to the person you think truly needs it.

Tell them that if someone who did not have even a grain of rice to chew some time back, someone who was told by his teachers to go home because his uniform was torn and dirty, someone who was always scolded by his boss at a computer shop or a hanger shop made it, so can you.

When I was alone in Gurgaon battling my wounds and circumstances, I was forging myself to reach the next level of being a strong man. Yes, I am strong, in fact such is the strength I have today that none can throw me down. Even if they succeed in doing so, you won't see me giving up. Till the very end of my life I am going to be a fighter.

Just to share with all of you, at the end of my life when I am on my death bed, I pray to be able to say this to myself with a smile on my face, "I have lived my life".

For friends I was a motivator, they sought my opinion when they most needed advice. You can only be a great friend when you don't expect anything out of your friend but do the needful to empower them to continue their walk.

Now I was not walking alone for my own goals anymore. I developed a self which was wanting to walk with more people and win over the adversities with synergy and cohesive efforts. This was tough, it was not in any way easy. In fact it is tougher to walk together with others, hand in hand, than walking the road all alone.

A walk has a bigger purpose that only you can fulfill. If you endure it you will certainly laugh at causes which wanted you to regress. Champions don't step back and so you won't because you are a champion too.

Tears roll down my face when I see someone suffering like I did. The thought that came to my mind was if only I could help him but then how would I do that? This idea of writing a book is solely for this purpose.

I met many friends who were very disturbed because of some problem or the other. For them it was all about being able to escape the issue or ignore it. Ignorance to me is a crime. It does not help in the long run. What if something you ignored now comes right in front of you sometime later? Will you do the same?

Only if you don't ignore the problem and find the courage to face issues head on will you be able to realize the mind blowing potential inherent in you. Somewhere, you will be forced to think and say, "Did I just do it? Yes, my friend, you did it." So, next time if you face a similar situation you won't back out like a coward. You will say, "Come on. I am ready to face it."

Wipe off those clouds of delusion from your mind and venture into the world of self-belief. This world can be made a better place if we in the first place, believe in our own potential.

The time did come when all of my patience, hard work and determination was to be answered. I had to see evidence that bore testimony to the meaning of the walk I endured for so long.

Comparing is something I have given up on. My mentor, the third president of the Buddhist group, the Soka Gakkai, namely Dr. Daisaku Ikeda says, "If you want to compare then compare yourself with what you were yesterday". Comparing oneself with another can bring only anxiety and feelings of inferiority for oneself.

I had become good friends with these two girls named Nitika and Smita. What is genuine friendship? I had this question answered then.

The placement season had begun.

I must admit that even I was anxious to get a placement with a good company at the earliest possible. When companies came for interviews I was determined to give my best first, without focusing much on the outcome. You see by now, you must have understood that I speak a lot to myself. Let me also share a secret with you, every morning when I wake up and sit down to chant my prayers, "Nam-Myoho-Renge-Kyo", I tell myself that I was born to win and be happy. Come what may I am going to give my best and not give up at all. Faith imbued with the spirit to be courageous slowly made my inner self stronger. Even my walk felt more confident than ever before. It said, "Yuvraj, keep forging ahead". I was feeling self confident like never before".

Let me share a secret with all of you. After incidents of heartbreaks in life I had made up my mind that I would never think of having a relationship in future. What I will do is only elevate my own life and grow with each single day.

I was very strict and rigid with myself. Despite this, I fell in love again. Yes I started liking a girl not for her looks but the innocent and joyful nature she possessed. I did not want her to know about my feelings because if she rejected my overtures I would feel hurt.

So, you see I am no super human, even I have fear but I have more faith than fear. While walking with her I would imagine how wonderful walking with her like this for the rest of our lives, would be.

Even if a part of me was very eager to be in a relationship with her, my desire to do the real big thing that mattered the most to me never took a back seat. My friends were awed to see me so focused. Some of my friends would say that my example would motivate them. During placements, I saw many of my friends feel shattered because they did not get through the interview of their dream company. The feeling for myself was the same. I wanted to get the best job with a handsome package so that I could go back home and tell my parents, "See mom and dad your son has turned his destiny and from now we are only going to live a better life than before".

I had sleepless nights when I thought about them. My entire being wanted to, and still wants them to, be enjoying the rest of their lives. While I felt so, I realized that there were some friends who had the same thing going in their minds. I then made it a point to stop thinking too much about my own goals and desires and do my best and in the process help my friends to do their best.

Today, none of them are in touch with me. Their other priorities have taken over. However, at the time I was willing to commit myself to a cohesive effort and see each one of us placed with a good company. I met them regularly and interacted with them and was always looking for ways through which we could get jobs in good companies. Doing this made me become a better human being as selfishness within me started being replaced with the feeling of compassion for all people around. It was like a period where I was enacting the drama of my life to the fullest. Someone who was once a sweeper, a cleaner and to put it bluntly, was a child with no hope for a good future was now a source of hope to all around him. I felt great. Those days when things would go awry, I would tell myself that someday people will know what I truly am and what my capabilities are.

I was witnessing all of it now. Sometimes at night when everyone else was asleep I would be awake to be alone and then try and constantly seek realization of my own weaknesses. In a way, I was wanting to become a perfectionist.

At the same time this girl started stealing my heart. I longed to see her once in a day. Her appearance was so innocent that it engendered the feeling of wanting to be with her for the rest of my life. Having been hurt before, I never wanted to hurt myself anymore.

Mentally I was forging myself so that if I heard a no from her end I could take it in my stride though I wished she would not decline my affection. But getting a placement was my priority so I kept my romantic feelings for my lady love quiet and continued to do what I had set my mind to.

Friends at college came to me when they needed some tips. I would do my best to motivate them. While doing so, I was myself becoming stronger.

I loved the strength I derived from my walk. It never let me stay low for long. When one of my friends did not get a job in a particular sector he was targeting, I pushed his negative thoughts aside and most importantly made him believe in himself. A guy who did not have friends or someone who always wanted people to talk to him was now being approached by every single student in college.

This episode in my life made me realize that I had in me what it takes to succeed. I was strong and had walked a long way since I had come to Calcutta aged 15. My walk became more intense as I wanted to reach my destination and then embark on another journey with a new destination altogether.

I have never had a moment where I have not experienced difficulty in being able to do things with ease. I have been scolded left and right by many people who were older and even younger than me. Yes, when all of this was happening, I would feel I was worthless.

Was I ready to accept it? Reality though was different from appearances. My entire being was eager to battle it out, all the time. I consider this life itself as a battle not against others but against our own weaknesses. I will not feel hesitant to reiterate this line, "At the end of the tunnel is light, the light of hope and the light of courage and everything that can brighten my life up. The only thing I must do is push myself either by walking or, if not walking, then by crawling and even if crawling does not help then by dragging myself. Believe me the level of empowerment you will witness is going to be amazing. In fact one will fall short of adjectives while describing it.

Even today, I feel disheartened about not being able to succeed at work or not being able to have a girlfriend. There are ample issues in life but what is it that really matters? It's the sheer belief and the walk which I've chosen to endure that makes me push myself a bit more every single time. If there is pain then there is a panacea for it too. However, the seminal question is – do I only want a solution to my pain or do I choose to use my pain as a cause for self growth.

Motivational talks can continue but what makes a difference is the bent of our hearts. If we communicate with people wholeheartedly encouraging new bonds of friendship to be formed then this world can become a wonderful place to live in.

No peace talks on an international level will help. What will help is heart to heart conversations. So, are you encouraging your friend to work hard for his dreams in a mechanical fashion or with a heart that sincerely cares for him?

During my placements, I was not just any other guy. I was a man who saw himself sitting for interviews with other students encouraging them to do their best. Giving them a shoulder to lean on was something that makes me proud even today. Can you ever imagine a guy who swept the floors of a shop was now a person who was helping others in their moment of grief?

What we see now is all through our naked eyes but what lies beyond it is unknown so let us together walk this walk of life with a sense of purpose towards our life and towards the common goal of bringing peace and harmony to ourselves and to those around us.

Every time my friends faced rejection I would still continue to push them forward and give them that one reason to give it their best shot. This pushed me to a different level altogether. Those friends are not in touch with me now but I'm sure they must remember me. Of course, I too wanted more friends and more fun with people around but I never had this opportunity. What I had was my sense of courage and hope that I could share with them.

Regarding job applications, I did not get through a lot of good companies. This shook my confidence. I started questioning my efforts to study diligently and work tirelessly to learn new things around me. I felt my hardwork and curiosity to learn were not paying off because I could not land a job. Every time I failed, I would come back to my room and cry my heart out. Yes, even with a history of dealing with hardships I had not developed a thick skin that could insulate me from feeling hurt about not securing a job. I wanted to do it just to make both my mother and my father proud of me. I strengthened my resolve to fight back and be victorious. When I say become victorious the idea of it is not confined to the goal of getting a job only but also includes infusing hope in my friends. My intention was now backed by a fiercely competitive attitude and this time I mentally prepared myself to get the offer letter in my hand by that evening.

During the course of my interview, I saw a recruiter not as a superior being or as someone inferior to me. Instead I saw him just as another human. This helped me in letting the interview become discussion oriented. When I left the interview room I was no longer that old and timid Yuvraj.

This was me unshakeable, wise, compassionate and full of enthusiasm believing strongly on one but very important point – that life is wonderful. This was a meaningful turn for me as I had never felt the joy I experienced after the interview got over.

Even then I did not get through. This failure acted as a spring board for me as I pumped my fist in the air and decided to not accept defeat. The walk I started at the age of 15 was now coming to an end. I wanted this ending to be a grand one. One that not only becomes a memory for me but a resource by virtue of which I could encourage people around me.

There was another company for which the interviews were ongoing and I was to appear for the final round with the CEO. I wanted to ease up a bit so I went out knowing that my turn would come last. I started smoking a couple of cigarettes. I wanted no one around me.

Thoughts started creeping in my head about how my entire life had unfolded and how things were on their way to becoming better. This walk was about to get over and I was a step closer to making it possible. Tears rolled down my cheeks but I was more determined this time. With lots of self-talking, I went into the interview room and the climax scene of A WALK began.

My breathing was becoming heavier and my emotions were running high. All that I had endured up till now started making me feel nostalgic. Suppressing these feelings for one last time was very important. I told myself, to this round I am going to give my absolute best. Once my interview started, I was all guns blazing. I was not answering any of my interviewer's questions. In fact, I was having a discussion with him on myriad contemporary topics.

That was it. The CEO told me during the interview itself that I was selected. I was in disbelief and twice asked him to repeat those lines. My joy knew no limits. When I was 15 everyone told me you will never be able to sell anything in life. You are simply good for nothing. That moment I had proved them wrong. Ecstatic and joyous I came out of the room and tightly hugged the girl I was in love with. I was keen to not only hug her but kiss her as well. But it did not happen that way. Holding her hand and coming back to my room, I felt I was now complete. The joy of getting a job and having her beside me made me so happy.

I was being driven by my emotions and once again I hugged her before she left for her room. I wished now I could tell her how I felt about her. I had helped her in discovering her smile and now it was me who wanted to hold her hand and be with her for the rest of my life.

You don't get all that you want but you do get things that you strive for with all your heart. The whole night

I was busy living those days of hardship which made me what I am today and felt better. This time, I did not need anyone to tap me. All alone, I walked this walk and the purpose which was so unclear then was now right in front of me.

Smita, the girl I had fallen in love with a few months ago never came to know about my love for her until I wrote a letter to her on the final day of college. It was also my last day in Delhi. My only wish was to hug her and see her smile for maybe one last time. This wish remained a wish only as she left for her home in Uttar Pradesh that very day itself.

Feeling sad and upset, I had the letter delivered to her through her friend and my other closest buddy, Nitika. Come what may, there were some people who always stood by me thinking of me as a very motivating person. Previously, I did not know I was capable of motivating others but now this has become the over-riding motive of my life.

I witnessed a great deal of difference in my attitude and behavior. It was not just my job that made me happy. It was my all-round development which made me feel more confident.

It never was easy but if I had given up, I would have never accomplished anything of this magnitude.

This walk has come to an end. It ended after 11 years. These 11 years have taught me more than any school could have taught me. Even if everything was on the negative side in life, I learnt to pick myself up and do what I was to do. Parents like mine are courageous enough to undergo many harsh trials in life yet see to it that their kids don't suffer. My parents, despite their own failures, kept me going. When I needed a shoulder to cry on, mom was there. Papa never showed emotions but his love and care for me will always be precious. Every single individual I encountered had a role to play in my life and they each played their parts – for which I whole heartedly thank them.

When I was returning back home after college was over, I wanted to share my story with the rest. No, I did not want to become a hero. I only wanted children, adolescents and young adults to believe in their walk. The walk you are walking is going to be amazing if you keep persevering and striving. Even if you don't see any ray of light, you must summon up that little bit of courage inside you to endure that very dark moment.

I feel your pain even if I have never met you. I understand failures more than anyone else. I know what it is like when a person you love breaks your heart. I know how not having enough money can compel you to get into the wrong things. In fact, this life is very beautiful. It teaches lessons of its own so that in the end we win. This win will comprise not only your success story but your overall dynamic growth which only you can witness.

Right from the day I developed rotten feet, I developed a deep friendship with my feet. My feet always made me move ahead. Even though I was doubtful if everything would be fine or not yet my feet, metaphorically and literally, wanted me to endure and keep pressing forward, each day believing that I would win and win comprehensively.

The lesson my life has taught me is very crucial and learning this took a lot out of me. I cried a lot in the playground or near a pond but somewhere my feet picked me up all the time. They wanted to push me each day. This is why, I emphasize words like perseverance and courage. What matters to me is that I did it in the end.

Right from working in a computer shop or approaching people for my education fees or being left heart broken by the girl I loved so much, all these experiences were testing moments for me. Yes, I did cry then but once my tears dried up I never looked back and kept walking. The whole idea is to make my readers believe in the mindset of continuing to persevere and to keep moving ahead. If today you were able to walk a mile then tomorrow walk an inch more but keep going, never give up is the central message.

Life is about growing each day. Succumbing to trivial issues of any kind is cowardice. It might seem to you that your problem is very big or nobody can understand the depth of it but you are wrong. Ask anyone around you if they are free of problems and the answer will be NO.

When you are being defeated by problems it is not the problem that is the problem. It is our own inability to solve the problem that is actually the problem. Therefore, it is imperative for all of us to nurture the spirit to continue even then. This does not mean that we should escape from the situation instead we must seek the courage within us which is dormant.

Reading my book and keeping it on the bookshelf is not going to help. Once you've read it, see if there is any one line that has touched your soul. If it has, then based on that very sentence become determined to stand firm when adversities assail you and continue to forge ahead.

While you continue don't expect things to be sorted soon. It is only 1) perseverance and 2) endurance which act as key ingredients in making this journey a memorable one. Like you don't leave your plate of food till you are full, similarly, don't ever forget to walk the walk you started and continue until you win like a champion.

My saying all of this is by no means a guarantee to a serene life. In fact until you don't make a resolve, even the simplest of things then will seem impossible.

I did not get the love of the girl I loved or maybe still love. It did hurt me a lot but not for long. I had a new walk to begin in life and doing that will always be my priority. In the process of following my belief system of perseverance I will perhaps attract my life partner along the way. When my teachers threw me out of school because of my torn uniform, my heart cried a lot but I could not express my feelings openly because there was no one around me to share my pain even fleetingly. When I was begging in front of people for money to study, I wanted to either die or again sit and cry because all of it, every moment made me feel hopeless. There was simply no ray of hope which could have made me feel lighter. My rotten feet understood my pain more than anybody else.

Had my feet not been in that state, I would not have been able to accomplish all that I have accomplished today. I am yet to grow and yet to achieve the impossible. This walk was incredibly fascinating. The courage I feel today is way more than it ever was.

Nothing seems to upset me for more than an hour. I need no one to come and pick me up or tap me when I am low. So, what do I do with such a story as mine? I have chosen to use my story to give hope to most of us who 'feel inferior or feel like life is so miserable to me only'.

There are many people around who have very serious issues in their lives. Often no one is there to hear them out. If you can share even a bit of my story with them I do pray and hope that they will see reason why they must not give up with their walk and why they must persevere with it.

Once they do so, hope will come alive not only in them but among people around them. Won't this world then become a world where peace and hope will triumph.

Only by self-reflecting day and night have I been able to decipher this theory and also realise the sole purpose of my life. Surely, it is through the implementation of this theory in our lives that we can not only challenge our own limitations and sorrows but also bring peace, hope and harmony in society in a true sense.

My system is more determined to smile everyday and see to it that no one around me is sad or low for long. Yes, that's how I am living my dream of making a positive difference to people around me.

A WALK is not a book for only men or women. It is a book that speaks to everyone. If I am to justify this statement one will surely not disagree with the fact that we all have hearts and emotions which are immensely powerful. At times, we do feel heart broken or disheartened when we fail or an unwanted situation arises.

Your story too can be the story of a hero. In fact, you are a hero. The only thing that is missing is the ability to realize this much needed fact in our lives. Ask your parents or anyone who you think loves and cares for you the most, a question, "Who is your Hero?" Certainly their answers will mention you. Yes, they will. More than anything else it's my conviction towards love and care for people around us that makes me say so.

Today when I am away from home nothing hurts or mellows me down. Even if it does, the belief system to continue lends me the courage to overcome my frailties and forge ahead. A unique sense of indestructible confidence builds within me. So, even if I have not been able to fulfill my goals and aspirations I am yet very determined to strive more the next day.

When I continue doing this each day, it becomes a habit. I love every bit of it. However, it is important for me and you to never seek isolation from people around us. They are very important for our growth. Have you ever made a sad face smile even for a second? Well, if you have done so then you must have felt that sense of joy and satisfaction in you which somehow makes you believe in the word called humanity.

I am an atheist and a true believer in being the reason for someone else's smile whilst continuing my walk. This not only brings a serene sense of joy that I witness in my life but also brings optimism with respect to the kind of future I strive towards each day. I thank all my misery and the bitter experiences from my childhood, they have truly helped me think more about humanity. They have helped me manifest a great deal of courage and compassion towards life.

If you think others to be the reason for your problems and continue to blame them and develop seeds of hatred the loss will be yours. Hurdles in life don't come to fulfill the purpose of making you a stone hearted individual. They come to tell you that humanity exists through you, through your compassion, through your courage. Let us cherish this gift that life has to offer us. Let us build a world where our children will find reason to love one another as compared to rushing to make judgments about people.

Doing all of this will take a lot out of you but will give you a future that is going to be filled with hope. Your tears are precious. They should only appear when you see others in pain. We must work on ourselves more than ever.

Only these small yet meaningful ways can bring compassion and peace into being and into the human experience. If someone around us is bad then let us not ignore them. Instead let us resolve to make them our best friend one day. Everything starts from a thought, an idea, so let us use them to bring smiles and joy all around. Our deeds like this will make people believe that every bit of their struggle is worth striving for.

A small argument or a brawl with anyone should not be allowed to impact our true nature as human beings. When we were kids we did not see people as either rich or poor. We saw each person as a human being only. If that was the case then why is it not the case now? Many of us would disagree because we believe, now more than ever, evil to be predominant in our society.

So how are we going to remove this evil from its roots? Is it by killing such people or by merely punishing them? Will doing this make peoples' lives better? Will we be able to tell our children that the world they live in is very peaceful and harmonious? There has to be an answer to this question. The answer is "YOU".

Everything in life depends on how you deal with situations and not how things have transpired for you. Let the adversities know that our lives are endowed with a purpose and none of it can bring you down.

There has never been a time more than now when courage and compassion have become a much sought after character in all of us. Let us develop such attributes every day. Our efforts to develop as compassionate and courageous men and women will assist us in doing good for humanity which would be free of any ulterior terms and conditions.

For those of us who seek a companion we must be wary of today's world. A fairy world of love has become a total illusion. It is okay to seek a companion but it becomes dangerous when our world gets centered around them only.

I too wanted love to be a fairy story but when my girlfriend made me feel useless I realized how wrong I was and how many valuable people in my life I ignored because of my wish to seek her love. Ever since then I have not forgotten my priorities and that is why when I started loving Smita, I had my priorities intact too.

A companion with whom you can look forward to the future with hope and who is a source of inspiration, encouraging you to push yourself to grow is a companion in the truest sense. Smita did not accept my love. I could have gone crazy and hurt myself more and more. Had I done that, then the book and my walk would not have been successful.

It has taken every single day's effort to complete this book. Even after work I made sure that I wrote at least a line if not a page.

Smita will always be a special girl to me. I seek her love even now but my parents need me too. I cannot become so self centered so as to forget my responsibilities.

If she has to be in my life, it is fine and if not, then that's also ok because it is my walk that is more important to me. One cannot believe the kind of strength and courage I get when I walk down the lane. I know that the journey is long but because it is long it is definitely going to be wonderful too. All of it is easier said than done and it will need constant valiant and determined efforts in every possible way. Even when faced with financial problems if you are able to comfort your family with your smile it is worth it for it brings hope which is more crucial than money itself.

To walk away from people and the stress that comes from dealing with people and to live in isolation might seem a great idea but in reality, in my view, it is no less than an act of cowardice. Your existence is for a profound purpose so continue your walk and enable others to do the same. Will this not help you in the growth of your own character?

I might be mighty pleased today but if I stick to the old moments of glory I am only going to dwell in the past. That walk is over and now there is another walk to be walked towards. I don't know what the destination is going to be like but I do know that this walk will be stronger than my previous one. Life is a journey and so is this walk. Till the very end of my life, I will continue to walk and make sure that when death beckons then without any regrets I will tell myself, "I lived my life".

Girls, be proud to be a girl for you all are truly the unsung heroines of your families. If men are to learn anything from women then it has to be their endurance and compassion. They don't get the credit they deserve. What they only want is their share of love and we as men must ensure that this one wish of theirs is met.

Without my mother I don't know if I would have been alive to witness this day. How can I forget that night when right outside Howrah Station my mother approached a relative of ours for money so that she could get my rotten feet treated? How can I forget her efforts of going to possibly all places in Calcutta to see to it that I could complete class 10? She has striven more than hard in making me a complete man. Today, when I look at her, the smile on her face says it all. How selfless women are, I ponder. So ladies out there feel confident about your inherent goodness. You make people like me stronger and more determined.

How can I give up when I know that my life purpose is yet to be fulfilled?

How can I say it's enough when I know I want to be the best and I'm still on the journey to being my best?

How can I say I don't care when I know I love the people around me?

Let's not cheat ourselves when we know that we want to be happy and win.

This thought expressed above is very close to my heart. Although I penned it spontaneously but all this while it has been my support system not allowing me to break down or consider myself worthless. Like a river that keeps flowing we must ignite our dormant courage to rise up and rise high.

No one else will ever know or maybe not even acknowledge the changes you are bringing in your life. It is your actions which will do the talking. So, before you give inputs to others, implement that very ideal in your own life. Believe me, you will develop much more depth in your life this way.

A WALK will possibly be my first and last book but I do hope that this book will inspire people. I am not a rich guy who can get things as he desires but I do have a character that can make a sad face smile.

Embrace difficulties with all your love. If I had realized and followed this before then possibly I would have been a greater person. You don't seem to be getting good marks, it is fine. You have no job to feed your family, it is also fine. You are always treated badly by your peers, it is fine even then. What is not fine is giving up on yourself.

I too had such moments and that too at an extreme level. Despite this, I did not want to accept defeat because I felt that everyone who has ridiculed me or done their bit in humiliating and discouraging me would be proven right. This was nothing but the attitude of never giving up at play and continuing the walk which led to a quiet, 'unputdownable' strength. Moving a step further, we must not treat these people who try to pull us down badly nor should we hold any grudges towards them. We must make them believe in us through our very own attitude of never giving up.

Some of us are not fortunate to be with our parents. So, does that mean you have missed out on something? No, in fact what you have gained is an opportunity to work more diligently, strengthen your character and better yourself as a person. Each of us understands life differently and hence the way you will understand life is different from others including me. Let the world learn from you through the struggles you have overcome because our times need more inspirational role models. Believe me, people like you have been entrusted with the wonderful mission of enabling humanity to better sustain its existence. However, seeing this opportunity as either a problem or a challenge is entirely your choice. Life without parents is like a house without a roof so would you not want to construct the roof of your own house through your own diligent efforts? You will have a lot to endure and there will certainly be many occasions when you want to cry to vent your frustration but you won't be able to.

Somewhere, your inner voice will keep telling you to keep pressing forward and that will be the best thing in your life, the realization of which will be there after a period of time and when there is no greater joy than being able to stand tall, all of your own making. The struggles of people when shared become an inspiration to other people to walk their walk on their own and make a future for themselves.

There was a gentleman I met when I was 18 years old studying in class 10. He happened to be a relative of ours. We met for the first time but to him it was as if he had known me since long. He looked me in the eye and said, "I see a lot of shine in your eyes and a lot of pain within you. Even then I want you to work diligently and never chose a path that appears to be very easy. You will definitely reach the top but you won't understand or cherish the value of being there."

His words left an indelible impression on me. I don't pray for things to become smoother for me. Instead, in my prayers I always wish to have as many hurdles as possible because I want to fashion myself to become a very capable individual. Come on, I am a champion, a hero who has fought since the age of 15 and there is nothing that can break my belief.

During your walk you will meet all kinds of people. Some might betray you and some will stay by your side. In either scenario be very thankful to both types of people because, believe it or not, these people are stepping stones leading you towards victory in the end. So, never hate them. As always, make a resolve to one day make them your closest friends.

Hatred towards anyone has done no good to anybody. It has only created walls of ego and mistrust. Even I am in a constant fight against my feelings of hatred towards people who have wronged me. Every single day, we must be determined to struggle valiantly yet develop a great deal of love and compassion for others. This way our very own walk can become a source for many to believe in – things like hope, light and belief for all, irrespective of what background they hail from.

Today I know what Cafe Coffee Day is, I know what Whatsapp is all about, I know the names of few car models, I also understand economics better than some of my college mates. I am earning well too. I feel joyous to have learnt things and to have done things I had always dreamt about. Above all, I understand the feelings of someone in pain much better than before. Being able to help and empower anyone in pain comes more naturally to me and I am proud of this trait that I have been able to develop over the years.

Now, a onetime sweeper comforts everyone around him. He speaks to his elders with a lot of concern. He does not tolerate any wrong doing of any kind whatsoever. I thank my 11 year journey because of which I have been able to identify and actualize the overarching purpose of my life.

I want to make sure all of us treat our current situation, whether good or bad, as a source to help bring peace and harmony in all our lives. So, are we ready to begin on this journey called, "A WALK"?

I want this book to end here only because now I want all of you, my lovely readers, to give a thumbs up to yourself and resolve to walk this walk and be victorious in bringing humanity alive. So, use this last page that I am leaving empty to write back to me about how are you planning to fight back and win.

Thank you so much for reading this story of mine. Hope we together do great things in life for the sake of humanity.

If you are going through various kinds of emotions,
feel free to share with me on my
Mail ID: yjain60@gmail.com